PRACTISING
THE POWER OF
NOW

PRACTISING THE POWER OF

NOW

Essential teachings,
meditations, and exercises
from *The Power of Now*

Eckhart Tolle

HODDER
MOBIUS

Copyright © 2001 by Eckhart Tolle

First published by New World Library, USA, in 2001

First published in Great Britain in 2002 by Hodder and Stoughton
A division of Hodder Headline

Most of the material in this book is excerpted from
The Power of Now © 1997 Eckhart Tolle

The right of Eckhart Tolle to be identified as the Author of the Work
has been asserted by him in accordance with the Copyright, Designs and
Patents Act 1988.

Text design: Mary Ann Casler
Typography: Tona Pearce Myers
Editing: Victoria Ritchie and Marc Allen

9

A CIP catalogue record for this title is available from the British Library

ISBN 978-1-444-70386-3

Printed and bound in Great Britain by
Clays Ltd, St Ives plc

Hodder and Stoughton
A division of Hodder Headline
338 Euston Road
London NW1 3BH

*The beginning of freedom is the realization
that you are not "the thinker."
The moment you start watching the thinker,
a higher level of consciousness becomes activated.
You then begin to realize that there is a vast realm
of intelligence beyond thought, that thought is only a
tiny aspect of that intelligence.
You also realize that all the things that truly matter —
beauty, love, creativity, joy, inner peace —
arise from beyond the mind.*

You begin to awaken.

CONTENTS

PART TWO

Relationship as Spiritual Practice

PART THREE

Acceptance and Surrender

INTRODUCTION

by Eckhart Tolle

Since it was first published in 1997, *The Power of Now* has already had an impact on the collective consciousness of the planet far beyond anything I could have imagined. It has been translated into fifteen languages, and I receive mail from around the globe every day from readers who tell me that their lives have been changed through coming into contact with the teaching embodied in the book.

Although the effects of the insanity of the egoic mind are still visible everywhere, something new *is* emerging. Never before have so many people been ready to break out of collective mind-patterns that have kept humanity in bondage to suffering since time immemorial. A new state of consciousness is emerging. We have suffered enough! Even at this moment it is emerging from within you, as you hold this book in your hands and read these lines that speak of the possibility of living the liberated life, in which you no longer inflict suffering on yourself or others.

Many of the readers who wrote to me expressed a wish to have the practical aspects of the teachings contained in *The Power of Now* presented in a more readily accessible format, to be used in their daily practice. That request became the impetus for this book.

In addition to the exercises and practices, however, this book also contains some shorter passages from the original work that can serve as a reminder of some of the ideas and concepts and can become a primer for incorporating those concepts daily.

Many of those passages are particularly suitable for meditative reading. When you practice meditative reading, you do not read primarily to gather new information, but to enter a different state of consciousness as you read. This is why you can re-read the same passage many times, and every time it feels fresh and new. Only words that were written or spoken in a state of presence have this transformative power, which is the power to awaken presence in the reader.

These passages are best read slowly. Many times

you may want to pause and allow for a moment of quiet reflection, or stillness. At other times, you may just open the book at random and read a few lines.

For those readers who felt daunted or overwhelmed by *The Power of Now,* this book can also serve as an introduction.

— Eckhart Tolle
July 9, 2001

PART ONE

*Accessing the
Power of Now*

When your consciousness
is directed outward,
mind and world arise.
When it is directed inward,
it realizes its own Source
and returns home into the Unmanifested.

ONE

❧

Being and Enlightenment

There is an eternal, ever-present One Life beyond the myriad forms of life that are subject to birth and death. Many people use the word God to describe it; I often call it Being. The word Being explains nothing, but nor does God. Being, however, has the advantage that it is an open concept. It does not reduce the infinite invisible to a finite entity. It is impossible to form a mental image of it. Nobody can claim exclusive possession of Being. It is your very presence, and it is immediately accessible to you as the feeling of your own presence. So it is only a small step from the word Being to the experience of Being.

BEING IS NOT ONLY BEYOND BUT ALSO DEEP WITHIN every form as its innermost invisible and indestructible essence. This means that it is accessible to you now as your own deepest self, your true nature. But don't seek to grasp it with your mind. Don't try to understand it.

You can know it only when the mind is still. When you are present, when your attention is fully and intensely in the Now, Being can be felt, but it can never be understood mentally.

To regain awareness of Being and to abide in that state of "feeling-realization" is enlightenment.

The word *enlightenment* conjures up the idea of some superhuman accomplishment, and the ego likes to keep it that way, but it is simply your natural state of felt oneness with Being. It is a state of connectedness with something immeasurable and indestructible, something that, almost paradoxically, is essentially you and yet is much greater than you. It is finding your true nature beyond name and form.

The inability to feel this connectedness gives rise to the illusion of separation, from yourself and from the world around you. You then perceive yourself, consciously or unconsciously, as an isolated fragment. Fear arises, and conflicts within and without become the norm.

The greatest obstacle to experiencing the reality of your connectedness is identification with your mind, which causes thought to become compulsive. Not to be able to stop thinking is a dreadful affliction, but we don't realize this because almost everybody is suffering from it, so it is considered normal. This incessant mental noise prevents you from finding that realm of inner stillness that is inseparable from Being. It also creates a false mind-made self that casts a shadow of fear and suffering.

Identification with your mind creates an opaque screen of concepts, labels, images, words, judgments, and definitions that blocks all true relationship. It comes between you and yourself, between you and your fellow man and woman, between you and nature, between you and God. It is this screen of thought that creates the illusion of separateness, the illusion that there is you and a totally separate "other." You then forget the essential fact that, underneath the level of physical appearances and separate forms, you are one with all that is.

The mind is a superb instrument if used rightly. Used wrongly, however, it becomes very destructive. To put it more accurately, it is not so much that you use your mind wrongly — you usually don't use it at all. It uses you. This is the disease. You believe that you are your mind. This is the delusion. The instrument has taken you over.

It's almost as if you were possessed without knowing it, and so you take the possessing entity to be yourself.

THE BEGINNING OF FREEDOM is the realization that you are not the possessing entity — the thinker. Knowing this enables you to observe the entity. The moment you start watching the thinker, a higher level of consciousness becomes activated.

You then begin to realize that there is a vast realm of intelligence beyond thought, that thought is only a tiny aspect of that intelligence. You also realize that all the things that truly matter — beauty, love, creativity, joy, inner peace — arise from beyond the mind.

You begin to awaken.

~

FREEING YOURSELF FROM YOUR MIND

The good news is that you can free yourself from your mind. This is the only true liberation. You can take the first step right now.

START LISTENING TO THE VOICE IN YOUR HEAD as often as you can. Pay particular attention to any repetitive thought patterns, those old audiotapes that have been playing in your head perhaps for many years.

This is what I mean by "watching the thinker," which is another way of saying: Listen to the voice in your head, be there as the witnessing presence.

When you listen to that voice, listen to it impartially. That is to say, do not judge. Do not judge or condemn what you hear, for doing so would mean that the same voice has come in again through the back door. You'll soon realize: There is the voice, and here I am listening to it, watching it. This *I am* realization, this sense of your own presence, is not a thought. It arises from beyond the mind.

So when you listen to a thought, you are aware not only of the thought but also of yourself as the witness of the thought. A new dimension of consciousness has come in.

AS YOU LISTEN TO THE THOUGHT, you feel a conscious presence — your deeper self — behind or underneath the thought, as it were. The thought then loses its power over you and quickly subsides, because you are no longer energizing the mind through identification with it. This is the beginning of the end of involuntary and compulsive thinking.

When a thought subsides, you experience a discontinuity in the mental stream — a gap of "no-mind." At first, the gaps will be short, a few seconds perhaps, but gradually they will become longer. When these gaps occur, you feel a certain stillness and peace inside you. This is the beginning of your natural state of felt oneness with Being, which is usually obscured by the mind.

With practice, the sense of stillness and peace will deepen. In fact, there is no end to its depth. You will also feel a subtle emanation of joy arising from deep within: the joy of Being.

In this state of inner connectedness, you are much more alert, more awake than in the mind-identified state. You are fully present. It also raises the vibrational frequency of the energy field that gives life to the physical body.

As you go more deeply into this realm of no-mind, as it is sometimes called in the East, you realize the state of pure consciousness. In that state, you feel your own presence with such intensity and such joy that all thinking, all emotions, your physical body, as well as the whole external world become relatively insignificant in comparison to it. And yet this is not a selfish but a selfless state. It takes you beyond what you previously thought of as "your self." That presence is essentially you and at the same time inconceivably greater than you.

INSTEAD OF "WATCHING THE THINKER," you can also create a gap in the mind stream simply by directing the focus of your attention into the Now. Just become intensely conscious of the present moment.

This is a deeply satisfying thing to do. In this way, you draw consciousness away from mind activity and create a gap of no-mind in which you are highly alert and aware but not thinking. This is the essence of meditation.

IN YOUR EVERYDAY LIFE, you can practice this by taking any routine activity that normally is only a means to an end and giving it your fullest attention, so that it becomes an end in itself. For example, every time you walk up and down the stairs in your house or place of work, pay close attention to every step, every movement, even your breathing. Be totally present.

Or when you wash your hands, pay attention to all the sense perceptions associated with the activity: the sound and feel of the water, the movement of your hands, the scent of the soap, and so on.

Or when you get into your car, after you close the door, pause for a few seconds and observe the flow of your breath. Become aware of a silent but powerful sense of presence.

There is one certain criterion by which you can measure your success in this practice: the degree of peace that you feel within.

The single most vital step on your journey toward enlightenment is this: Learn to disidentify from your mind. Every time you create a gap in the stream of mind, the light of your consciousness grows stronger.

One day you may catch yourself smiling at the voice in your head, as you would smile at the antics of a child. This means that you no longer take the content of your mind all that seriously, as your sense of self does not depend on it.

~

ENLIGHTENMENT: RISING ABOVE THOUGHT

As you grow up, you form a mental image of who you are, based on your personal and cultural conditioning. We may call this phantom self the ego. It consists of mind activity and can only be kept going through constant thinking. The term *ego* means different things to different people, but when I use it here it means a false self, created by unconscious identification with the mind.

To the ego, the present moment hardly exists. Only past and future are considered important. This total reversal of the truth accounts for the fact that in the ego mode the mind is so dysfunctional. It is always concerned with keeping the past alive, because without it — who are you? It constantly projects itself into the future to ensure its continued survival and to seek some kind of release or fulfillment there. It says: "One day, when this, that, or the other happens, I am going to be okay, happy, at peace."

Even when the ego seems to be concerned with the present, it is not the present that it sees: It misperceives it completely because it looks at it through the eyes of the past. Or it reduces the present to a means to an end, an end that always lies in the mind-projected future. Observe your mind and you'll see that this is how it works.

The present moment holds the key to liberation. But you cannot find the present moment as long as you are your mind.

Enlightenment means rising above thought. In the enlightened state, you still use your thinking mind when needed, but in a much more focused and effective way than before. You use it mostly for practical purposes, but you are free of the involuntary internal dialogue, and there is inner stillness.

When you do use your mind, and particularly when a creative solution is needed, you oscillate every few minutes or so between thought and stillness, between mind and no-mind. No-mind is consciousness without thought. Only in that way is it possible to think creatively, because only in that way does thought have any real power. Thought alone, when it is no longer connected with the much vaster realm of consciousness quickly becomes barren, insane, destructive.

∽

EMOTION:
THE BODY'S REACTION TO YOUR MIND

Mind, in the way I use the word, is not just thought. It includes your emotions as well as all unconscious mental-emotional reactive patterns. Emotion arises at the place where mind and body meet. It is the body's reaction to your mind — or you might say a reflection of your mind in the body.

The more you are identified with your thinking, your likes and dislikes, judgments and interpretations, which is to say the less present you are as the watching consciousness, the stronger the emotional energy charge will be, whether you are aware of it or not. If you cannot feel your emotions, if you are cut off from them, you will eventually experience them on a purely physical level, as a physical problem or symptom.

IF YOU HAVE DIFFICULTY FEELING YOUR EMOTIONS, start by focusing attention on the inner energy field of your body. Feel the body from within. This will also put you in touch with your emotions.

If you really want to know your mind, the body will always give you a truthful reflection, so look at the emotion, or rather feel it in your body. If there is an apparent conflict between them, the thought will be the lie, the emotion will be the truth. Not the ultimate truth of who you are, but the relative truth of your state of mind at that time.

You may not yet be able to bring your unconscious mind activity into awareness as thoughts, but it will always be reflected in the body as an emotion, and of this you can become aware.

To watch an emotion in this way is basically the same as listening to or watching a thought, which I described earlier. The only difference is that, while a thought is in your head, an emotion has a strong physical component and so is primarily felt in the body. You can then allow the emotion to be there without being controlled by it. You no longer are the emotion; you are the watcher, the observing presence.

If you practice this, all that is unconscious in you will be brought into the light of consciousness.

MAKE IT A HABIT TO ASK YOURSELF: What's going on inside me at this moment? That question will point you in the right direction. But don't analyze, just watch. Focus your attention within. Feel the energy of the emotion.

If there is no emotion present, take your attention more deeply into the inner energy field of your body. It is the doorway into Being.

TWO

The Origin of Fear

The psychological condition of fear is divorced from any concrete and true immediate danger. It comes in many forms: unease, worry, anxiety, nervousness, tension, dread, phobia, and so on. This kind of psychological fear is always of something that might happen, not of something that is happening now. You are in the here and now, while your mind is in the future. This creates an anxiety gap. And if you are identified with your mind and have lost touch with the power and simplicity of the Now, that anxiety gap will be your constant companion. You can always cope with the present moment, but you cannot cope with something that is only a mind projection — you cannot cope with the future.

Moreover, as long as you are identified with your mind, the ego runs your life. Because of its phantom nature, and despite elaborate defense mechanisms, the ego is very vulnerable and insecure, and it sees itself as constantly under threat. This, by the way, is the case even if the ego is outwardly very confident. Now remember that an emotion is the body's reaction to your mind. What message is the body receiving continuously from the ego, the false, mind-made self? Danger, I am under threat. And what is the emotion generated by this continuous message? Fear, of course.

Fear seems to have many causes. Fear of loss, fear of failure, fear of being hurt, and so on, but ultimately all fear is the ego's fear of death, of annihilation. To the ego, death is always just around the corner. In this mind-identified state, fear of death affects every aspect of your life.

For example, even such a seemingly trivial and "normal" thing as the compulsive need to be right in an argument and make the other person wrong — defending the mental position with which you have identified — is due to the fear of death. If you identify with a mental position, then if you are wrong, your mind-based sense of self is seriously threatened with annihilation. So you as the ego cannot afford to be wrong. To be wrong is to die. Wars have been fought over this, and countless relationships have broken down.

Once you have disidentified from your mind, whether you are right or wrong makes no difference to your sense of self at all, so the forcefully compulsive and deeply unconscious need to be right, which is a form of violence, will no longer be there. You can state clearly and firmly how you feel or what you think, but there will be no aggressiveness or defensiveness about it. Your sense of self is then derived from a deeper and truer place within yourself, not from the mind.

WATCH OUT FOR ANY KIND OF DEFENSIVENESS within yourself. What are you defending? An illusory identity, an image in your mind, a fictitious entity. By making this pattern conscious, by witnessing it, you disidentify from it. In the light of your consciousness, the unconscious pattern will then quickly dissolve.

This is the end of all arguments and power games, which are so corrosive to relationships. Power over others is weakness disguised as strength. True power is within, and it is available to you now.

The mind always seeks to deny the Now and to escape from it. In other words, the more you are identified with your mind, the more you suffer. Or you may put it like this: The more you are able to honor and accept the Now, the more you are free of pain, of suffering — and free of the egoic mind.

If you no longer want to create pain for yourself and others, if you no longer want to add to the residue of past pain that still lives on in you, then don't create any more time, or at least no more than is necessary to deal with the practical aspects of your life. How to stop creating time?

REALIZE DEEPLY THAT THE PRESENT MOMENT is all you ever have. Make the Now the primary focus of your life.

Whereas before you dwelt in time and paid brief visits to the Now, have your dwelling place in the Now and pay brief visits to past and future when required to deal with the practical aspects of your life situation.

Always say "yes" to the present moment.

❧

END THE DELUSION OF TIME

Here is the key: End the delusion of time. Time and mind are inseparable. Remove time from the mind and it stops — unless you choose to use it.

To be identified with your mind is to be trapped in time: the compulsion to live almost exclusively through memory and anticipation. This creates an endless preoccupation with past and future and an unwillingness to honor and acknowledge the present moment and allow it to be. The compulsion arises because the past gives you an identity and the future holds the promise of salvation, of fulfillment in whatever form. Both are illusions.

The more you are focused on time — past and future — the more you miss the Now, the most precious thing there is.

Why is it the most precious thing? Firstly, because it is the only thing. It's all there is. The eternal present is the space within which your whole life unfolds, the one factor that remains constant. Life is now. There was never a time when your life was not now, nor will there ever be.

Secondly, the Now is the only point that can take you beyond the limited confines of the mind. It is your only point of access into the timeless and formless realm of Being.

Have you ever experienced, done, thought, or felt anything outside the Now? Do you think you ever will? Is it possible for anything to happen or be outside the Now? The answer is obvious, is it not?

Nothing ever happened in the past; it happened in

the Now. Nothing will ever happen in the future; it will happen in the Now.

The essence of what I am saying here cannot be understood by the mind. The moment you grasp it, there is a shift in consciousness from mind to Being, from time to presence. Suddenly, everything feels alive, radiates energy, emanates Being.

THREE

～

Entering the Now

With the timeless dimension comes a different kind of knowing, one that does not "kill" the spirit that lives within every creature and every thing. A knowing that does not destroy the sacredness and mystery of life but contains a deep love and reverence for all that is. A knowing of which the mind knows nothing.

BREAK THE OLD PATTERN of present-moment denial and present-moment resistance. Make it your practice to withdraw attention from past and future whenever they are not needed. Step out of the time dimension as much as possible in everyday life.

If you find it hard to enter the Now directly, start by observing the habitual tendency of your mind to want to escape from the Now. You will observe that the future is usually imagined as either better or worse than the present. If the imagined future is better, it gives you hope or pleasurable anticipation. If it is worse, it creates anxiety. Both are illusory.

Through self-observation, more presence comes into your life automatically. The moment you realize you are not present, you are present. Whenever you are able to observe your mind, you are no longer trapped in it. Another factor has come in, something that is not of the mind: the witnessing presence.

Be present as the watcher of your mind — of your thoughts and emotions as well as your reactions in various situations. Be at least as interested in your reactions as in the situation or person that causes you to react.

Notice also how often your attention is in the past or future. Don't judge or analyze what you observe. Watch the thought, feel the emotion, observe the reaction. Don't make a personal problem out of them. You will then feel something more powerful than any of those things that you observe: the still, observing presence itself behind the content of your mind, the silent watcher.

Intense presence is needed when certain situations trigger a reaction with a strong emotional charge, such as when your self-image is threatened, a challenge comes into your life that triggers fear, things "go wrong," or an emotional complex from the past is brought up. In those instances, the tendency is for you to become "unconscious." The reaction or emotion takes you over — you "become" it. You act it out. You justify, make wrong, attack, defend... except that it isn't you, it's the reactive pattern, the mind in its habitual survival mode.

Identification with the mind gives it more energy; observation of the mind withdraws energy from it. Identification with the mind creates more time; observation of the mind opens up the dimension of the timeless. The energy that is withdrawn from the mind turns into presence. Once you can feel what it means to be present, it becomes much easier to simply choose to step out of the time dimension whenever time is not needed for practical purposes and move more deeply into the Now.

This does not impair your ability to use time — past or future — when you need to refer to it for practical matters. Nor does it impair your ability to use your mind. In fact, it enhances it. When you do use your mind, it will be sharper, more focused.

The enlightened person's main focus of attention is always the Now, but they are still peripherally aware of time. In other words, they continue to use clock time but are free of psychological time.

$\sim$

LETTING GO OF PSYCHOLOGICAL TIME

Learn to use time in the practical aspects of your life — we may call this "clock time" — but immediately return to present-moment awareness when those practical matters have been dealt with. In this way, there will be no buildup of "psychological time," which is identification with the past and continuous compulsive projection into the future.

If you set yourself a goal and work toward it, you are using clock time. You are aware of where you want to go, but you honor and give your fullest attention to the step that you are taking at this moment. If you then become excessively focused on the goal, perhaps because you are seeking happiness, fulfillment, or a more complete sense of self in it, the Now is no longer honored. It becomes reduced to a mere stepping-stone to the future, with no intrinsic value. Clock time then turns into psychological time. Your life's journey is no longer an adventure, just an obsessive need to arrive, to attain, to "make it." You no longer see or smell the flowers by the wayside either, nor are you aware of the beauty and the miracle of life that unfolds all around you when you are present in the Now.

Are you always trying to get somewhere other than where you are? Is most of your doing just a means to an end? Is fulfillment always just around the corner or confined to short-lived pleasures, such as sex, food, drink, drugs, or thrills and excitement? Are you always focused on becoming, achieving, and attaining, or alternatively chasing some new thrill or pleasure? Do you believe that if you acquire more things you will become more fulfilled, good enough, or psychologically complete? Are you waiting for a man or woman to give meaning to your life?

In the normal, mind-identified or unenlightened state of consciousness, the power and infinite creative potential that lie concealed in the Now are completely obscured by psychological time. Your life then loses its vibrancy, its freshness, its sense of wonder. The old patterns of thought, emotion, behavior, reaction, and desire are acted out in endless repeat performances, a script in your mind that gives you an identity of sorts but distorts or covers up the reality of the Now. The mind then creates an obsession with the future as an escape from the unsatisfactory present.

What you perceive as future is an intrinsic part of

your state of consciousness now. If your mind carries a heavy burden of past, you will experience more of the same. The past perpetuates itself through lack of presence. The quality of your consciousness at this moment is what shapes the future — which, of course, can only be experienced as the Now.

If it is the quality of your consciousness at this moment that determines the future, then what is it that determines the quality of your consciousness? Your degree of presence. So the only place where true change can occur and where the past can be dissolved is the Now.

You may find it hard to recognize that time is the cause of your suffering or your problems. You believe that they are caused by specific situations in your life, and seen from a conventional viewpoint, this is true. But until you have dealt with the basic problem-making dysfunction of the mind — its attachment to past and future and denial of the Now — problems are actually interchangeable.

If all your problems or perceived causes of suffering or unhappiness were miraculously removed for you today, but you had not become more present, more conscious, you would soon find yourself with a similar set of problems or causes of suffering, like a shadow that follows you wherever you go. Ultimately, there is only one problem: the time-bound mind itself.

There is no salvation in time. You cannot be free in the future.

PRESENCE IS THE KEY to freedom, so you can only be free now.

~

FINDING THE LIFE UNDERNEATH YOUR LIFE SITUATION

What you refer to as your "life" should more accurately be called your "life situation." It is psychological time: past and future. Certain things in the past didn't go the way you wanted them to go. You are still resisting what happened in the past, and now you are resisting what is. Hope is what keeps you going, but hope keeps you focused on the future, and this continued focus perpetuates your denial of the Now and therefore your unhappiness.

FORGET ABOUT YOUR LIFE SITUATION for a while and pay attention to your life.

Your life situation exists in time. Your life is now.

Your life situation is mind-stuff. Your life is real.

Find the "narrow gate that leads to life." It

is called the Now. Narrow your life down to this moment. Your life situation may be full of problems — most life situations are — but find out if you have any problem at this moment. Not tomorrow or in ten minutes, but now. Do you have a problem now?

When you are full of problems, there is no room for anything new to enter, no room for a solution. So whenever you can, make some room, create some space, so that you find the life underneath your life situation.

USE YOUR SENSES FULLY. Be where you are. Look around. Just look, don't interpret. See the light, shapes, colors, textures. Be aware of the silent presence of each thing. Be aware of the space that allows everything to be.

Listen to the sounds; don't judge them. Listen to the silence underneath the sounds.

Touch something — anything — and feel and acknowledge its Being.

Observe the rhythm of your breathing; feel the air flowing in and out, feel the life energy inside your body. Allow everything to be, within and without. Allow the "isness" of all things. Move deeply into the Now.

You are leaving behind the deadening world of mental abstraction, of time. You are getting out of the insane mind that is draining you of life energy, just as it is slowly poisoning and destroying the Earth. You are awakening out of the dream of time into the present.

∽

ALL PROBLEMS ARE ILLUSIONS OF THE MIND

FOCUS YOUR ATTENTION ON THE NOW and tell me what problem you have at this moment.

I am not getting any answer because it is impossible to have a problem when your attention is fully in the Now. A situation needs to be either dealt with or accepted. Why make it into a problem?

The mind unconsciously loves problems because they give you an identity of sorts. This is normal, and it is insane. "Problem" means that you are dwelling on a situation mentally without there being a true intention or possibility of taking action now and that you are unconsciously making it part of your sense of self. You become so overwhelmed by your life situation that you lose your sense of life, of Being. Or you are carrying in your mind the insane burden of a hundred things that you will or may have to do in the future instead of focusing your attention on the one thing that you can do now.

> **WHEN YOU CREATE A PROBLEM,** you create pain. All it takes is a simple choice, a simple decision: No matter what happens, I will create no more pain for myself. I will create no more problems.

Although it is a simple choice, it is also very radical. You won't make that choice unless you are truly fed up with suffering, unless you have truly had enough. And you won't be able to go through with it unless you access the power of the Now. If you create no more pain for yourself, then you create no more pain for others. You also no longer contaminate the beautiful Earth, your inner space, and the collective human psyche with the negativity of problem making.

Should a situation arise that you need to deal with now, your action will be clear and incisive if it arises out of present-moment awareness. It is also more likely to be effective. It will not be a reaction coming from the past conditioning of your mind but an intuitive response to the situation. In other instances, when the time-bound mind would have reacted, you will find it more effective to do nothing — just stay centered in the Now.

~

THE JOY OF BEING

To alert you that you have allowed yourself to be taken over by psychological time, you can use a simple criterion.

ASK YOURSELF: Is there joy, ease, and lightness in what I am doing? If there isn't, then time is covering up the present moment, and life is perceived as a burden or a struggle.

If there is no joy, ease, or lightness in what you are doing, it does not necessarily mean that you need to change what you are doing. It may be sufficient to change the how. "How" is always more important than "what." See if you can give much more attention to the doing than to the result that you want to achieve through it. Give your fullest attention to whatever the moment presents. This implies that you also completely accept what is, because you cannot give your full attention to something and at the same time resist it.

As soon as you honor the present moment, all unhappiness and struggle dissolve, and life begins to flow with joy and ease. When you act out of present-moment awareness, whatever you do becomes imbued with a sense of quality, care, and love — even the most simple action.

DO NOT BE CONCERNED WITH THE FRUIT OF YOUR ACTION — just give attention to the action itself. The fruit will come of its own accord. This is a powerful spiritual practice.

When the compulsive striving away from the Now ceases, the joy of Being flows into everything you do. The moment your attention turns to the Now, you feel a presence, a stillness, a peace. You no longer depend on the future for fulfillment and satisfaction — you don't look to it for salvation. Therefore, you are not attached to the results. Neither failure nor success has the power to change your inner state of Being. You have found the life underneath your life situation.

In the absence of psychological time, your sense of self is derived from Being, not from your personal past. Therefore, the psychological need to become anything other than who you are already is no longer there. In the world, on the level of your life situation, you may indeed become wealthy, knowledgeable, successful, free of this or that, but in the deeper dimension of Being you are complete and whole now.

❧

THE TIMELESS STATE OF CONSCIOUSNESS

When every cell of your body is so present that it feels vibrant with life, and when you can feel that life every moment as the joy of Being, then it can be said that you are free of time. To be free of time is to be free of the psychological need of the past for your identity and the future for your fulfillment. It represents the most profound transformation of consciousness that you can imagine.

WHEN YOU HAVE HAD YOUR FIRST FEW GLIMPSES OF THE TIMELESS STATE OF CONSCIOUSNESS, you begin to move back and forth between the dimensions of time and presence. First you become aware of just how rarely your attention is truly in the Now. But to know that you are not present is a great success: That knowing is presence — even if initially it only lasts for a couple of seconds of clock time before it is lost again.

Then, with increasing frequency, you choose to have the focus of your consciousness in the present moment rather than in the past or future, and whenever you realize that you had lost the Now, you are able to stay in it not just for a couple of seconds, but for longer periods as perceived from the external perspective of clock time.

So before you are firmly established in the state of presence, which is to say, before you are fully conscious, you shift back and forth for a while between consciousness and unconsciousness, between the state of presence and the state of mind identification. You lose the Now, and you return to it, again and again. Eventually, presence becomes your predominant state.

FOUR

❦

Dissolving Unconciousness

It is essential to bring more consciousness into your life in ordinary situations when everything is going relatively smoothly. In this way, you grow in presence power. It generates an energy field in you and around you of a high vibrational frequency. No unconsciousness, no negativity, no discord or violence can enter that field and survive, just as darkness cannot survive in the presence of light.

When you learn to be the witness of your thoughts and emotions, which is an essential part of being present, you may be surprised when you first become aware of the background "static" of ordinary unconsciousness and realize how rarely, if ever, you are truly at ease within yourself.

On the level of your thinking, you will find a great deal of resistance in the form of judgment, discontent, and mental projection away from the Now. On the emotional level, there will be an undercurrent of unease, tension, boredom, or nervousness. Both are aspects of the mind in its habitual resistance mode.

OBSERVE THE MANY WAYS IN WHICH UNEASE, discontent, and tension arise within you through unnecessary judgment, resistance to what is, and denial of the Now.

Anything unconscious dissolves when you shine the light of consciousness on it.

Once you know how to dissolve ordinary unconsciousness, the light of your presence will shine brightly, and it will be much easier to deal with deep unconsciousness whenever you feel its gravitational pull. However, ordinary unconsciousness may not be easy to detect initially because it is so normal.

MAKE IT A HABIT TO MONITOR YOUR MENTAL AND EMOTIONAL STATE through self-observation.

"Am I at ease at this moment?" is a good question to ask yourself frequently.

Or you can ask: "What's going on inside me at this moment?"

Be at least as interested in what goes on inside you as what happens outside. If you get the inside right, the outside will fall into place. Primary reality is within, secondary reality without.

BUT DON'T ANSWER THESE QUESTIONS IMMEDIATELY. Direct your attention inward. Have a look inside yourself.

What kind of thoughts is your mind producing?

What do you feel?

Direct your attention into the body. Is there any tension?

Once you detect that there is a low level of unease, the background static, see in what way you are avoiding, resisting, or denying life — by denying the Now.

There are many ways in which people unconsciously resist the present moment. With practice, your power of self-observation, of monitoring your inner state, will become sharpened.

～

WHEREVER YOU ARE, BE THERE TOTALLY

Are you stressed? Are you so busy getting to the future that the present is reduced to a means of getting there? Stress is caused by being "here" but wanting to be "there," or being in the present but wanting to be in the future. It's a split that tears you apart inside.

Does the past take up a great deal of your attention? Do you frequently talk and think about it, either positively or negatively? The great things that you have achieved, your adventures or experiences, or your victim story and the dreadful things that were done to you, or maybe what you did to someone else?

Are your thought processes creating guilt, pride, resentment, anger, regret, or self-pity? Then you are not only reinforcing a false sense of self but also helping to accelerate your body's aging process by creating an accumulation of past in your psyche. Verify this for yourself by observing those around you who have a strong tendency to hold on to the past.

DIE TO THE PAST EVERY MOMENT. You don't need it. Only refer to it when it is absolutely relevant to the present. Feel the power of this moment and the fullness of Being. Feel your presence.

Are you worried? Do you have many "what if" thoughts? You are identified with your mind, which is projecting itself into an imaginary future situation and creating fear. There is no way that you can cope with such a situation, because it doesn't exist. It's a mental phantom.

You can stop this health- and life-corroding insanity simply by acknowledging the present moment.

> **BECOME AWARE OF YOUR BREATHING.** Feel the air flowing in and out of your body. Feel your inner energy field. All that you ever have to deal with, cope with, in real life — as opposed to imaginary mind projections — is this moment.
>
> Ask yourself what "problem" you have right now, not next year, tomorrow, or five minutes from now. What is wrong with this moment?

You can always cope with the Now, but you can never cope with the future — nor do you have to. The answer, the strength, the right action, or the resource will be there when you need it, not before, not after.

Are you a habitual "waiter"? How much of your life do you spend waiting? What I call "small-scale waiting" is waiting in line at the post office, in a traffic jam, at the airport, or waiting for someone to arrive, to finish work, and so on. "Large-scale waiting" is waiting for the next vacation, for a better job, for the children to grow up, for a truly meaningful relationship, for success, to make money, to be important, to become enlightened. It is not uncommon for people to spend their whole life waiting to start living.

Waiting is a state of mind. Basically, it means that you want the future; you don't want the present. You don't want what you've got, and you want what you haven't got. With every kind of waiting, you unconsciously create inner conflict between your here and now, where you don't want to be, and the projected future, where you want to be. This greatly reduces the quality of your life by making you lose the present.

For example, many people are waiting for prosperity. It cannot come in the future. When you honor, acknowledge, and fully accept your present reality — where you are, who you are, what you are doing right now — when you fully accept what you have got, you are grateful for what you have got, grateful for what is, grateful for Being. Gratitude for the present moment and the fullness of life now is true prosperity. It cannot come in the future. Then, in time, that prosperity manifests for you in various ways.

If you are dissatisfied with what you have got, or even frustrated or angry about your present lack, that may motivate you to become rich, but even if you do make millions, you will continue to experience the inner condition of lack, and deep down you will continue to feel unfulfilled. You may have many exciting experiences that money can buy, but they will come and go and always leave you with an empty feeling and the need for further physical or psychological gratification. You won't abide in Being and so feel the fullness of life now that alone is true prosperity.

GIVE UP WAITING AS A STATE OF MIND. When you catch yourself slipping into waiting...snap out of it. Come into the present moment. Just be, and enjoy being. If you are present, there is never any need for you to wait for anything.

So next time somebody says, "Sorry to have kept you waiting," you can reply, "That's all right, I wasn't waiting. I was just standing here enjoying myself — in joy in my self."

These are just a few of the habitual mind strategies for denying the present moment that are part of ordinary unconsciousness. They are easy to overlook because they are so much a part of normal living: the background static of perpetual discontent. But the more you practice monitoring your inner mental-emotional state, the easier it will be to know when you have been trapped in past or future, which is to say unconscious, and to awaken out of the dream of time into the present.

But beware: The false, unhappy self, based on mind identification, lives on time. It knows that the present moment is its own death and so feels very threatened by it. It will do all it can to take you out of it. It will try to keep you trapped in time.

In a sense, the state of presence could be compared to waiting. It is a qualitatively different kind of waiting, one that requires your total alertness. Something could happen at any moment, and if you are not absolutely awake, absolutely still, you will miss it. In that state, all your attention is in the Now. There is none left for daydreaming, thinking, remembering, anticipating. There is no tension in it, no fear, just alert presence. You are present with your whole Being, with every cell of your body.

In that state, the "you" that has a past and a future, the personality if you like, is hardly there anymore. And yet nothing of value is lost. You are still essentially yourself. In fact, you are more fully yourself than you ever were before, or rather it is only now that you are truly yourself.

❧

THE PAST CANNOT SURVIVE
IN YOUR PRESENCE

Whatever you need to know about the unconscious past in you, the challenges of the present will bring it out. If you delve into the past, it will become a bottomless pit: There is always more. You may think that you need more time to understand the past or become free of it, in other words, that the future will eventually free you of the past. This is a delusion. Only the present can free you of the past. More time cannot free you of time.

Access the power of Now. That is the key. The power of Now is none other than the power of your presence, your consciousness liberated from thought forms. So deal with the past on the level of the present. The more attention you give to the past, the more you energize it, and the more likely you are to make a "self" out of it.

Don't misunderstand: Attention is essential, but not to the past as past. Give attention to the present; give attention to your behavior, to your reactions, moods, thoughts, emotions, fears, and desires as they occur in the present. There's the past in you. If you can be present enough to watch all those things, not critically or analytically but nonjudgmentally, then you are dealing with the past and dissolving it through the power of your presence.

You cannot find yourself by going into the past.
You find yourself by coming into the present.

FIVE

❧

Beauty Arises in the Stillness of Your Presence

Presence is needed to become aware of the beauty, the majesty, the sacredness of nature. Have you ever gazed up into the infinity of space on a clear night, awestruck by the absolute stillness and inconceivable vastness of it? Have you listened, truly listened, to the sound of a mountain stream in the forest? Or to the song of a blackbird at dusk on a quiet summer evening?

To become aware of such things, the mind needs to be still. You have to put down for a moment your personal baggage of problems, of past and future, as well as all your knowledge; otherwise, you will see but not see, hear but not hear. Your total presence is required.

BEYOND THE BEAUTY OF THE EXTERNAL FORMS, there is more here: something that cannot be named, something ineffable, some deep, inner, holy essence. Whenever and wherever there is beauty, this inner essence shines through somehow. It only reveals itself to you when you are present.

Could it be that this nameless essence and your presence are one and the same?

Would it be there without your presence?

Go deeply into it. Find out for yourself.

∾

REALIZING PURE CONSCIOUSNESS

Whenever you watch the mind, you withdraw consciousness from mind forms, which then becomes what we call the watcher or the witness. Consequently, the watcher — pure consciousness beyond form — becomes stronger, and the mental formations become weaker.

When we talk about watching the mind, we are personalizing an event that is truly of cosmic significance: Through you, consciousness is awakening out of its dream of identification with form and withdrawing from form. This foreshadows, but is already part of, an event that is probably still in the distant future as far as chronological time is concerned. The event is called — the end of the world.

TO STAY PRESENT IN EVERYDAY LIFE, it helps to be deeply rooted within yourself; otherwise, the mind, which has incredible momentum, will drag you along like a wild river.

It means to inhabit your body fully. To always have some of your attention in the inner energy field of your body. To feel the body from within, so to speak. Body awareness keeps you present. It anchors you in the Now.

The body that you can see and touch cannot take you into Being. But that visible and tangible body is only an outer shell, or rather a limited and distorted perception of a deeper reality. In your natural state of connectedness with Being, this deeper reality can be felt every moment as the invisible inner body, the animating presence within you. So to "inhabit the body" is to feel the body from within, to feel the life inside the body and thereby come to know that you are beyond the outer form.

You are cut off from Being as long as your mind takes up all your attention. When this happens — and it happens continuously for most people — you are not in your body. The mind absorbs all your consciousness and transforms it into mind stuff. You cannot stop thinking.

To become conscious of Being, you need to reclaim

consciousness from the mind. This is one of the most essential tasks on your spiritual journey. It will free vast amounts of consciousness that previously had been trapped in useless and compulsive thinking. A very effective way of doing this is simply to take the focus of your attention away from thinking and direct it into the body, where Being can be felt in the first instance as the invisible energy field that gives life to what you perceive as the physical body.

∼

CONNECTING WITH THE INNER BODY

Please try it now. You may find it helpful to close your eyes for this practice. Later on, when "being in the body" has become natural and easy, this will no longer be necessary.

> **DIRECT YOUR ATTENTION INTO THE BODY.** Feel it from within. Is it alive? Is there life in your hands, arms, legs, and feet — in your abdomen, your chest?
>
> Can you feel the subtle energy field that pervades the entire body and gives vibrant life to every organ and every cell? Can you feel it simultaneously in all parts of the body as a single field of energy?

Keep focusing on the feeling of your inner body for a few moments. Do not start to think about it. Feel it.

The more attention you give it, the clearer and stronger this feeling will become. It will feel as if every cell is becoming more alive, and if you have a strong visual sense, you may get an image of your body becoming luminous. Although such an image can help you temporarily, pay more attention to the feeling than to any image that may arise. An image, no matter how beautiful or powerful, is already defined in form, so there is less scope for penetrating more deeply.

∽

GOING DEEPLY INTO THE BODY

To go even more deeply into the body, try the following meditation. Ten to fifteen minutes of clock time should be sufficient.

MAKE SURE FIRST THAT THERE ARE NO EXTERNAL DISTRACTIONS such as telephones or people who are likely to interrupt you. Sit on a chair, but don't lean back. Keep the spine erect. Doing so will help you to stay alert. Alternatively, choose your own favorite position for meditation.

Make sure the body is relaxed. Close your eyes. Take a few deep breaths. Feel yourself breathing into the lower abdomen, as it were. Observe how it expands and contracts slightly with each in and out breath.

Then become aware of the entire inner energy field of the body. Don't think about it — feel it. By doing this, you reclaim consciousness from the mind. If you find it helpful, use the "light" visualization I just described.

When you can feel the inner body clearly as a single field of energy, let go, if possible, of any visual image and focus exclusively on the feeling. If you can, also drop any mental image you may still have of the physical body. All that is left then is an all-encompassing sense of presence or "beingness," and the inner body is felt to be without a boundary.

Then take your attention even more deeply into that feeling. Become one with it. Merge with the energy field, so that there is no longer a perceived duality of the observer and the observed, of you and your body. The distinction between inner and outer also dissolves now, so there is no inner body anymore. By going deeply into the body, you have transcended the body.

Stay in this realm of pure Being for as long as feels comfortable; then become aware again of the physical body, your breathing and physical senses, and open your eyes. Look at your surroundings for a few minutes in a meditative way — that is, without labeling them mentally — and continue to feel the inner body as you do so.

Having access to that formless realm is truly liberating. It frees you from bondage to form and identification with form. We may call it the Unmanifested, the invisible Source of all things, the Being within all beings. It is a realm of deep stillness and peace, but also of joy and intense aliveness. Whenever you are present, you become "transparent" to some extent to the light, the pure consciousness that emanates from this Source. You also realize that the light is not separate from who you are but constitutes your very essence.

When your consciousness is directed outward, mind and world arise. When it is directed inward, it realizes its own Source and returns home into the Unmanifested.

Then, when your consciousness comes back to the manifested world, you reassume the form identity that you temporarily relinquished. You have a name, a past, a life situation, a future. But in one essential respect, you are not the same person you were before: You will have glimpsed a reality within yourself that is not "of this world," although it isn't separate from it, just as it isn't separate from you.

Now let your spiritual practice be this:

AS YOU GO ABOUT YOUR LIFE, don't give 100 percent of your attention to the external world and to your mind. Keep some within.

Feel the inner body even when engaged in everyday activities, especially when engaged in relationships or when you are relating with nature. Feel the stillness deep inside it. Keep the portal open.

It is quite possible to be conscious of the Unmanifested throughout your life. You feel it as a deep sense of peace somewhere in the background, a stillness that never leaves you, no matter what happens out here. You become a bridge between the Unmanifested and the manifested, between God and the world.

This is the state of connectedness with the Source that we call enlightenment.

$\backsim$

HAVE DEEP ROOTS WITHIN

The key is to be in a state of permanent connectedness with your inner body — to feel it at all times. This will rapidly deepen and transform your life. The more consciousness you direct into the inner body, the higher its vibrational frequency becomes, much like a light that grows brighter as you turn up the dimmer switch and so increase the flow of electricity. At this higher energy level, negativity cannot affect you anymore, and you tend to attract new circumstances that reflect this higher frequency.

If you keep your attention in the body as much as possible, you will be anchored in the Now. You won't lose yourself in the external world, and you won't lose yourself in your mind. Thoughts and emotions, fears and desires may still be there to some extent, but they won't take you over.

PLEASE EXAMINE WHERE YOUR ATTENTION IS at this moment. You are listening to me, or you are reading these words in a book. That is the focus of your attention. You are also peripherally aware of your surroundings, other people, and so on. Furthermore, there may be some mind activity around what you are hearing or reading, some mental commentary.

Yet there is no need for any of this to absorb all your attention. See if you can be in touch with your inner body at the same time. Keep some of your attention within. Don't let it all flow out. Feel your whole body from within, as a single field of energy. It is almost as if you were listening or reading with your whole body. Let this be your practice in the days and weeks to come.

Do not give all your attention away to the mind and the external world. By all means focus on what you are doing, but feel the inner body at the same time whenever possible. Stay rooted within. Then observe how this changes your state of consciousness and the quality of what you are doing.

Please don't just accept or reject what I am saying. Put it to the test.

~

STRENGTHENING THE IMMUNE SYSTEM

There is a simple but powerful self-healing meditation that you can do whenever you feel the need to boost your immune system. It is particularly effective if used when you feel the first symptoms of an illness, but it also works with illnesses that are already entrenched if you use it at frequent intervals and with an intense focus. It will also counteract any disruption of your energy field by some form of negativity.

It is not a substitute, however, for the moment-to-moment practice of being in the body; otherwise, its effect will only be temporary. Here it is.

WHEN YOU ARE UNOCCUPIED FOR A FEW MINUTES, and especially last thing at night before falling asleep and first thing in the morning before getting up, "flood" your body with consciousness. Close your eyes. Lie flat on your back. Choose different parts of your body to focus your attention on briefly at first: hands, feet, arms, legs, abdomen, chest, head, and so on. Feel the life energy inside those parts as intensely as you can. Stay with each part for fifteen seconds or so.

Then let your attention run through the body like a wave a few times, from feet to head and back again. This need only take a minute or so. After that, feel the inner body in its totality, as a single field of energy. Hold that feeling for a few minutes.

Be intensely present during that time, present in every cell of your body.

Don't be concerned if the mind occasionally succeeds in drawing your attention out of the body and you lose yourself in some thought. As soon as you notice that this has happened, just return your attention to the inner body.

~

CREATIVE USE OF MIND

If you need to use your mind for a specific purpose, use it in conjunction with your inner body. Only if you are able to be conscious without thought can you use your mind creatively, and the easiest way to enter that state is through your body.

WHENEVER AN ANSWER, A SOLUTION, OR A CREATIVE IDEA IS NEEDED, stop thinking for a moment by focusing attention on your inner energy field. Become aware of the stillness.

When you resume thinking, it will be fresh and creative. In any thought activity, make it a habit to go back and forth every few minutes or so between thinking and an inner kind of listening, an inner stillness.

We could say: Don't just think with your head, think with your whole body.

~

LET THE BREATH TAKE YOU INTO THE BODY

If at any time you are finding it hard to get in touch with the inner body, it is usually easier to focus on your breathing first. Conscious breathing, which is a powerful meditation in its own right, will gradually put you in touch with the body.

FOLLOW THE BREATH WITH YOUR ATTENTION as it moves in and out of your body. Breathe into the body, and feel your abdomen expanding and contracting slightly with each inhalation and exhalation.

If you find it easy to visualize, close your eyes and see yourself surrounded by light or immersed in a luminous substance — a sea of consciousness. Then breathe in that light. Feel that luminous substance filling up your body and making it luminous also.

Then gradually focus more on the feeling. Don't get attached to any visual image. You are now in your body. You have accessed the power of Now.

PART TWO

Relationship
as Spiritual
Practice

Love is a state of Being.
Your love is not outside; it is deep within you.
You can never lose it, and it cannot leave you.
It is not dependent on some other body,
some external form.

SIX

Dissolving the Pain-body

The greater part of human pain is unnecessary. It is self-created as long as the unobserved mind runs your life. The pain that you create now is always some form of nonacceptance, some form of unconscious resistance to what is.

On the level of thought, the resistance is some form of judgment. On the emotional level, it is some form of negativity. The intensity of the pain depends on the degree of resistance to the present moment, and this in turn depends on how strongly you are identified with your mind. The mind always seeks to deny the Now and to escape from it.

In other words, the more you are identified with your mind, the more you suffer. Or you may put it like this: The more you are able to honor and accept the Now, the more you are free of pain, of suffering — and free of the egoic mind.

Some spiritual teachings state that all pain is ultimately an illusion, and this is true. The question is: Is it true for you? A mere belief doesn't make it true. Do you want to experience pain for the rest of your life and keep saying that it is an illusion? Does that free you from the pain? What we are concerned with here is how you can realize this truth — that is, make it real in your own experience.

Pain is inevitable as long as you are identified with your mind, which is to say as long as you are unconscious, spiritually speaking. I am talking here primarily of emotional pain, which is also the main cause of physical pain and physical disease. Resentment, hatred, self-pity, guilt, anger, depression, jealousy, and so on, even the slightest irritation, are all forms of pain. And every pleasure or emotional high contains within itself the seed of pain: its inseparable opposite, which will manifest in time.

Anybody who has ever taken drugs to get "high" will know that the high eventually turns into a low, that the pleasure turns into some form of pain. Many people also know from their own experience how easily and quickly an intimate relationship can turn from a source of pleasure to a source of pain. Seen from a higher perspective, both the negative and the positive polarities are faces of the same coin, are part of the underlying pain that is inseparable from the mind-identified egoic state of consciousness.

There are two levels to your pain: the pain that you create now, and the pain from the past that still lives on in your mind and body.

As long as you are unable to access the power of the Now, every emotional pain that you experience leaves behind a residue of pain that lives on in you. It merges with the pain from the past, which was already there, and becomes lodged in your mind and body. This, of course, includes the pain you suffered as a child, caused by the unconsciousness of the world into which you were born.

This accumulated pain is a negative energy field that occupies your body and mind. If you look on it as an invisible entity in its own right, you are getting quite close to the truth. It's the emotional pain-body.

The pain-body has two modes of being: dormant and active. It may be dormant 90 percent of the time; in a deeply unhappy person, though, it may be active up to 100 percent of the time. Some people live almost entirely through their pain-body, while others may

experience it only in certain situations, such as intimate relationships, or situations linked with past
loss or abandonment, physical or emotional hurt, and
so on.

Anything can trigger it, particularly if it resonates
with a pain pattern from your past. When it is ready to
awaken from its dormant stage, even a thought or an
innocent remark made by someone close to you can
activate it.

~

BREAKING IDENTIFICATION
WITH THE PAIN-BODY

**THE PAIN-BODY DOESN'T WANT YOU TO OBSERVE
IT DIRECTLY** and see it for what it is. The
moment you observe the pain-body, feel its
energy field within you, and take your attention into it, the identification is broken.

A higher dimension of consciousness has
come in. I call it presence. You are now the witness or the watcher of the pain-body. This
means that it cannot use you anymore by pretending to be you, and it can no longer replen-
ish itself through you. You have found your
own innermost strength.

Some pain-bodies are obnoxious but relatively harmless, for example, like a child who won't stop whining. Others are vicious and destructive monsters, true demons. Some are physically violent; many more are emotionally violent. Some will attack people around you or close to you, while others may attack you, their host. Thoughts and feelings you have about your life then become deeply negative and self-destructive. Illnesses and accidents are often created in this way. Some pain-bodies drive their hosts to suicide.

When you thought you knew a person and then you are suddenly confronted with this alien, nasty creature for the first time, you are in for quite a shock. It is more important, however, to observe it in yourself than in someone else.

WATCH OUT FOR ANY SIGN OF UNHAPPINESS IN YOURSELF, in whatever form — it may be the awakening pain-body. This can take the form of irritation, impatience, a somber mood, a desire to hurt, anger, rage, depression, a need to have some drama in your relationship, and so on. Catch it the moment it awakens from its dormant state.

The pain-body wants to survive, just like every other entity in existence, and it can only survive if it gets you to unconsciously identify with it. It can then rise up, take you over, "become you," and live through you.

It needs to get its "food" through you. It will feed on any experience that resonates with its own kind of energy, anything that creates further pain in whatever form: anger, destructiveness, hatred, grief, emotional drama, violence, and even illness. So the pain-body, when it has taken you over, will create a situation in your life that reflects back its own energy frequency for it to feed on. Pain can only feed on pain. Pain cannot feed on joy. It finds it quite indigestible.

Once the pain-body has taken you over, you want more pain. You become a victim or a perpetrator. You want to inflict pain, or you want to suffer pain, or both. There isn't really much difference between the two. You are not conscious of this, of course, and will vehemently claim that you do not want pain. But look closely and you will find that your thinking and behavior are designed to keep the pain going, for yourself and others. If you were truly conscious of it, the pattern would dissolve, for to want more pain is insanity, and nobody is consciously insane.

The pain-body, which is the dark shadow cast by the ego, is actually afraid of the light of your consciousness. It is afraid of being found out. Its survival depends on your unconscious identification with it, as well as on your unconscious fear of facing the pain that lives in you. But if you don't face it, if you don't bring the light of your consciousness into the pain, you will be forced to relive it again and again.

The pain-body may seem to you like a dangerous monster that you cannot bear to look at, but I assure you that it is an insubstantial phantom that cannot prevail against the power of your presence.

WHEN YOU BECOME THE WATCHER and start to disidentify, the pain-body will continue to operate for a while and will try to trick you into identifying with it again. Although you are no longer energizing it through your identification, it has a certain momentum, just like a spinning wheel that will keep turning for a while even when it is no longer being propelled. At this stage, it may also create physical aches and pains in different parts of the body, but they won't last.

Stay present, stay conscious. Be the ever-alert guardian of your inner space. You need to be present enough to be able to watch the pain-body directly and feel its energy. It then cannot control your thinking.

The moment your thinking is aligned with the energy field of the pain-body, you are identified with it and again feeding it with your thoughts. For example, if anger is the predominant energy vibration of the pain-body and you think angry thoughts, dwelling on what someone did to you or what you are going to do to him or her, then you have become unconscious, and the pain-body has become "you." Where there is anger, there is always pain underneath.

Or when a dark mood comes upon you and you start getting into a negative mind-pattern and thinking how dreadful your life is, your thinking has become aligned with the pain-body, and you have become unconscious and vulnerable to the pain-body's attack.

"Unconscious," the way that I use the word here, means to be identified with some mental or emotional pattern. It implies a complete absence of the watcher.

❧

TRANSMUTING SUFFERING INTO CONSCIOUSNESS

Sustained conscious attention severs the link between the pain-body and your thought processes and brings about the process of transmutation. It is as if the pain becomes fuel for the flame of your consciousness, which then burns more brightly as a result.

This is the esoteric meaning of the ancient art of alchemy: the transmutation of base metal into gold, of suffering into consciousness. The split within is healed, and you become whole again. Your responsibility then is not to create further pain.

FOCUS ATTENTION ON THE FEELING INSIDE YOU. Know that it is the pain-body. Accept that it is there. Don't think about it — don't let the feeling turn into thinking. Don't judge or analyze. Don't make an identity for yourself out of it. Stay present, and continue to be the observer of what is happening inside you.

Become aware not only of the emotional pain but also of "the one who observes," the silent watcher. This is the power of the Now, the power of your own conscious presence. Then see what happens.

∾

EGO IDENTIFICATION WITH THE PAIN-BODY

The process that I have just described is profoundly powerful yet simple. It could be taught to a child, and hopefully one day it will be one of the first things children learn in school. Once you have understood the basic principle of being present as the watcher of what happens inside you — and you "understand" it by experiencing it — you have at your disposal the most potent transformational tool.

This is not to deny that you may encounter intense inner resistance to disidentifying from your pain. This will be the case particularly if you have lived closely identified with your emotional pain-body for most of your life and the whole or a large part of your sense of self is invested in it. What this means is that you have made an unhappy self out of your pain-body and believe that this mind-made fiction is who you are. In that case, unconscious fear of losing your identity will create strong resistance to any disidentification. In other words, you would rather be in pain — be the pain-body — than take a leap into the unknown and risk losing the familiar unhappy self.

OBSERVE THE RESISTANCE WITHIN YOURSELF.

Observe the attachment to your pain. Be very alert. Observe the peculiar pleasure you derive from being unhappy. Observe the compulsion to talk or think about it. The resistance will cease if you make it conscious.

You can then take your attention into the pain-body, stay present as the witness, and so initiate its transmutation.

Only you can do this. Nobody can do it for you. But if you are fortunate enough to find someone who is intensely conscious, if you can be with them and join them in the state of presence, that can be helpful and will accelerate things. In this way, your own light will quickly grow stronger.

When a log that has only just started to burn is placed next to one that is burning fiercely, and after a while they are separated again, the first log will be burning with much greater intensity. After all, it is the same fire. To be such a fire is one of the functions of a spiritual teacher. Some therapists may also be able to fulfill that function, provided that they have gone beyond the level of mind and can create and sustain a state of intense conscious presence while they are working with you.

The first thing to remember is this: As long as you make an identity for yourself out of the pain, you cannot become free of it. As long as part of your sense of self is invested in your emotional pain, you will unconsciously resist or sabotage every attempt that you make to heal that pain.

Why? Quite simply because you want to keep yourself intact, and the pain has become an essential part of you. This is an unconscious process, and the only way to overcome it is to make it conscious.

∽

THE POWER OF YOUR PRESENCE

TO SUDDENLY SEE that you are or have been attached to your pain can be quite a shocking realization. The moment you realize this, you have broken the attachment.

The pain-body is an energy field, almost like an entity, that has become temporarily lodged in your inner space. It is life energy that has become trapped, energy that is no longer flowing.

Of course, the pain-body is there because of certain things that happened in the past. It is the living past in you, and if you identify with it, you identify with the past. A victim identity is the belief that the past is more powerful than the present, which is the opposite of the truth. It is the belief that other people and what they did to you are responsible for who you are now, for your emotional pain or your inability to be your true self.

The truth is that the only power there is, is contained within this moment: It is the power of your presence. Once you know that, you also realize that you are responsible for your inner space now — nobody else is — and that the past cannot prevail against the power of the Now.

Unconsciousness creates it; consciousness transmutes it into itself. St. Paul expressed this universal principle beautifully: "Everything is shown up by being exposed to the light, and whatever is exposed to the light itself becomes light."

Just as you cannot fight the darkness, you cannot fight the pain-body. Trying to do so would create inner conflict and thus further pain. Watching it is enough. Watching it implies accepting it as part of what is at that moment.

SEVEN

❧

From Addictive to Enlightened Relationships

LOVE/HATE RELATIONSHIPS

Unless and until you access the consciousness frequency of presence, all relationships, and particularly intimate relationships, are deeply flawed and ultimately dysfunctional. They may seem perfect for a while, such as when you are "in love," but invariably that apparent perfection gets disrupted as arguments, conflicts, dissatisfaction, and emotional or even physical violence occur with increasing frequency.

It seems that most "love relationships" become love/hate relationships before long. Love can then turn into savage attack, feelings of hostility, or complete withdrawal of affection at the flick of a switch. This is considered normal.

If in your relationships you experience both "love" and the opposite of love — attack, emotional violence, and so on — then it is likely that you are confusing ego attachment and addictive clinging with love. You cannot love your partner one moment and attack him or her the next. True love has no opposite. If your "love" has an opposite, then it is not love but a strong ego-need for a more complete and deeper sense of self, a need that the other person temporarily meets. It is the ego's substitute for salvation, and for a short time it almost does feel like salvation.

But there comes a point when your partner behaves in ways that fail to meet your needs, or rather those of your ego. The feelings of fear, pain, and lack that are an intrinsic part of egoic consciousness but had been covered up by the "love relationship" now resurface.

Just as with every other addiction, you are on a high when the drug is available, but invariably there comes a time when the drug no longer works for you.

When those painful feelings reappear, you feel them even more strongly than before, and what is more, you now perceive your partner as the cause of those feelings. This means that you project them outward and attack the other with all the savage violence that is part of your pain.

This attack may awaken the partner's own pain, and he or she may counter your attack. At this point, the ego is still unconsciously hoping that its attack or its attempts at manipulation will be sufficient punishment to induce your partner to change their behavior, so that it can use them again as a cover-up for your pain.

Every addiction arises from an unconscious refusal to face and move through your own pain. Every addiction starts with pain and ends with pain. Whatever the substance you are addicted to — alcohol, food, legal or illegal drugs, or a person — you are using something or somebody to cover up your pain.

That is why, after the initial euphoria has passed, there is so much unhappiness, so much pain in intimate relationships. They do not cause pain and unhappiness. They bring out the pain and unhappiness that is already in you. Every addiction does that. Every addiction reaches a point where it does not work for you anymore, and then you feel the pain more intensely than ever.

This is one reason why most people are always trying to escape from the present moment and are seeking some kind of salvation in the future. The first thing that they might encounter if they focused their attention on the Now is their own pain, and this is what they fear. If they only knew how easy it is to access in the Now the power of presence that dissolves the past and its pain, the reality that dissolves the illusion. If they only knew how close they are to their own reality, how close to God.

Avoidance of relationships in an attempt to avoid pain is not the answer either. The pain is there anyway. Three failed relationships in as many years are more likely to force you into awakening than three years on a desert island or shut away in your room. But if you could bring intense presence into your aloneness, that would work for you too.

~

FROM ADDICTIVE TO ENLIGHTENED RELATIONSHIPS

WHETHER YOU ARE LIVING ALONE OR WITH A PARTNER, this remains the key: being present and intensifying your presence by taking your attention ever more deeply into the Now.

For love to flourish, the light of your presence needs to be strong enough so that you no longer get taken over by the thinker or the pain-body and mistake them for who you are.

To know yourself as the Being underneath the thinker, the stillness underneath the mental noise, the love and joy underneath the pain, is freedom, salvation, enlightenment.

To disidentify from the pain-body is to bring presence into the pain and thus transmute it. To disidentify from thinking is to be the silent watcher of your thoughts and behavior, especially the repetitive patterns of your mind and the roles played by the ego.

If you stop investing it with "selfness," the mind loses its compulsive quality, which basically is the compulsion to judge, and so to resist what is, which creates conflict, drama, and new pain. In fact, the moment that judgment stops through acceptance of what is, you are free of the mind. You have made room for love, for joy, for peace.

FIRST YOU STOP JUDGING YOURSELF; then you stop judging your partner. The greatest catalyst for change in a relationship is complete acceptance of your partner as he or she is, without needing to judge or change them in any way.

That immediately takes you beyond ego. All mind games and all addictive clinging are then over. There are no victims and no perpetrators anymore, no accuser and accused.

This is also the end of all codependency, of being drawn into somebody else's unconscious pattern and thereby enabling it to continue. You will then either separate — in love — or move ever more deeply into the Now together, into Being. Can it be that simple? Yes, it is that simple.

Love is a state of Being. Your love is not outside; it is deep within you. You can never lose it, and it cannot leave you. It is not dependent on some other body, some external form.

> **IN THE STILLNESS OF YOUR PRESENCE,** you can feel your own formless and timeless reality as the unmanifested life that animates your physical form. You can then feel the same life deep within every other human and every other creature. You look beyond the veil of form and separation. This is the realization of oneness. This is love.

Although brief glimpses are possible, love cannot flourish unless you are permanently free of mind identification and your presence is intense enough to have dissolved the pain-body — or you can at least remain present as the watcher. The pain-body cannot then take you over and so become destructive of love.

~

RELATIONSHIPS AS SPIRITUAL PRACTICE

As humans have become increasingly identified with their mind, most relationships are not rooted in Being and so turn into a source of pain and become dominated by problems and conflict.

If relationships energize and magnify egoic mind patterns and activate the pain-body, as they do at this time, why not accept this fact rather than try to escape from it? Why not cooperate with it instead of avoiding relationships or continuing to pursue the phantom of an ideal partner as an answer to your problems or a means of feeling fulfilled?

With the acknowledgment and acceptance of the facts also comes a degree of freedom from them.

For example, when you *know* there is disharmony and you hold that "knowing," through your knowing a new factor has come in, and the disharmony cannot remain unchanged.

WHEN YOU KNOW YOU ARE NOT AT PEACE, your knowing creates a still space that surrounds your nonpeace in a loving and tender embrace and then transmutes your nonpeace into peace.

As far as inner transformation is concerned, there is nothing you can *do* about it. You cannot transform yourself, and you certainly cannot transform your partner or anybody else. All you *can* do is create a space for transformation to happen, for grace and love to enter.

So whenever your relationship is not working, whenever it brings out the "madness" in you and in your partner, be glad. What was unconscious is being brought up to the light. It is an opportunity for salvation.

EVERY MOMENT, HOLD THE KNOWING OF THAT MOMENT, particularly of your inner state. If there is anger, know that there is anger. If there is jealousy, defensiveness, the urge to argue, the need to be right, an inner child demanding love and attention, or emotional pain of any kind — whatever it is, know the reality of that moment and hold the knowing.

The relationship then becomes your sadhana, your spiritual practice. If you observe unconscious behavior in your partner, hold it in the loving embrace of your knowing so that you won't react.

Unconsciousness and knowing cannot coexist for long — even if the knowing is only in the other person and not in the one who is acting out the unconsciousness. The energy form that lies behind hostility and attack finds the presence of love absolutely intolerable. If you react at all to your partner's unconsciousness, you become unconscious yourself. But if you then remember to know your reaction, nothing is lost.

Never before have relationships been as problematic and conflict ridden as they are now. As you may have noticed, they are not here to make you happy or fulfilled. If you continue to pursue the goal of salvation through a relationship, you will be disillusioned again and again. But if you accept that the relationship is here to make you conscious instead of happy, then the relationship will offer you salvation, and you will be aligning yourself with the higher consciousness that wants to be born into this world.

For those who hold on to the old patterns, there will be increasing pain, violence, confusion, and madness.

How many people does it take to make your life into a spiritual practice? Never mind if your partner will not cooperate. Sanity — consciousness — can only come into this world through you. You do not need to wait for the world to become sane, or for somebody else to become conscious, before you can be enlightened. You may wait forever.

Do not accuse each other of being unconscious. The moment you start to argue, you have identified with a mental position and are now defending not only that position but also your sense of self. The ego is in charge. You have become unconscious. At times, it may be appropriate to point out certain aspects of your partner's behavior. If you are very alert, very present, you can do so without ego involvement — without blaming, accusing, or making the other wrong.

When your partner behaves unconsciously, relinquish all judgment. Judgment is either to confuse someone's unconscious behavior with who they are or to project your own unconsciousness onto another person and mistake that for who they are.

To relinquish judgment does not mean that you do not recognize dysfunction and unconsciousness when you see it. It means "being the knowing" rather than "being the reaction" and the judge. You will then either be totally free of reaction or you may react and still be the knowing, the space in which the reaction is watched and allowed to be. Instead of fighting the darkness, you bring in the light. Instead of reacting to delusion, you see the delusion yet at the same time look through it.

Being the knowing creates a clear space of loving presence that allows all things and all people to be as they are. No greater catalyst for transformation exists. If you practice this, your partner cannot stay with you and remain unconscious.

If you both agree that the relationship will be your spiritual practice, so much the better. You can then express your thoughts and feelings to each other as soon as they occur, or as soon as a reaction comes up, so that you do not create a time gap in which an unexpressed or unacknowledged emotion or grievance can fester and grow.

> **LEARN TO GIVE EXPRESSION** to what you feel without blaming. Learn to listen to your partner in an open, nondefensive way.
>
> Give your partner space for expressing himself or herself. Be present. Accusing, defending, attacking — all those patterns that are designed to strengthen or protect the ego or to get its needs met will then become redundant. Giving space to others — and to yourself — is vital. Love cannot flourish without it.

When you have removed the two factors that are destructive of relationships — when the pain-body has been transmuted and you are no longer identified with mind and mental positions — and if your partner has done the same, you will experience the bliss of the flowering of relationship. Instead of mirroring to each other your pain and your unconsciousness, instead of satisfying your mutual addictive ego needs, you will reflect back to each other the love that you feel deep within, the love that comes with the realization of your oneness with all that is.

This is the love that has no opposite.

If your partner is still identified with the mind and

the pain-body while you are already free, this will represent a major challenge — not to you but to your partner. It is not easy to live with an enlightened person, or rather it is so easy that the ego finds it extremely threatening.

Remember that the ego needs problems, conflict, and "enemies" to strengthen the sense of separateness on which its identity depends. The unenlightened partner's mind will be deeply frustrated because its fixed positions are not resisted, which means they will become shaky and weak, and there is even the "danger" that they may collapse altogether, resulting in loss of self.

The pain-body is demanding feedback and not getting it. The need for argument, drama, and conflict is not being met.

~

GIVE UP THE RELATIONSHIP WITH YOURSELF

Enlightened or not, you are either a man or a woman, so on the level of your form identity you are not complete. You are one-half of the whole. This incompleteness is felt as male-female attraction, the pull toward the opposite energy polarity, no matter how conscious you are. But in that state of inner connectedness, you feel this pull somewhere on the surface or periphery of your life.

This does not mean that you don't relate deeply to other people or to your partner. In fact, you can relate deeply only if you are conscious of Being. Coming from Being, you are able to focus beyond the veil of form. In Being, male and female are one. Your form may continue to have certain needs, but Being has none. It is already complete and whole. If those needs are met, that is beautiful, but whether or not they are met makes no difference to your deep inner state.

So it is perfectly possible for an enlightened person, if the need for the male or female polarity is not met, to feel a sense of lack or incompleteness on the outer level of his or her being, yet at the same time be totally complete, fulfilled, and at peace within.

If you cannot be at ease with yourself when you are alone, you will seek a relationship to cover up your unease. You can be sure that the unease will then reappear in some other form within the relationship, and you will probably hold your partner responsible for it.

ALL YOU REALLY NEED TO DO IS ACCEPT THIS MOMENT FULLY. You are then at ease in the here and now and at ease with yourself.

But do you need to have a relationship with yourself at all? Why can't you just be yourself? When you have a relationship with yourself, you have split yourself into two: "I" and "myself," subject and object. That mind-created duality is the root cause of all unnecessary complexity, of all problems and conflict in your life.

In the state of enlightenment, you are yourself — "you" and "yourself" merge into one. You do not judge yourself, you do not feel sorry for yourself, you are not proud of yourself, you do not love yourself, you do not hate yourself, and so on. The split caused by self-reflective consciousness is healed, its curse removed. There is no "self" that you need to protect, defend, or feed anymore.

When you are enlightened, there is one relationship that you no longer have: the relationship with yourself. Once you have given that up, all your other relationships will be love relationships.

PART THREE

~

Acceptance and Surrender

When you surrender to what is
and so become fully present,
the past ceases to have any power.
The realm of Being, which had been obscured by
the mind, then opens up.
Suddenly, a great stillness arises within you,
an unfathomable sense of peace.
And within that peace, there is great joy.
And within that joy, there is love.
And at the innermost core, there is the sacred,
the immeasurable, That which cannot be named.

EIGHT

❧

Acceptance of the Now

IMPERMANENCE AND THE CYCLES OF LIFE

There are cycles of success, when things come to you and thrive, and cycles of failure, when they wither or disintegrate, and you have to let them go in order to make room for new things to arise, or for transformation to happen.

If you cling and resist at that point, it means you are refusing to go with the flow of life, and you will suffer. Dissolution is needed for new growth to happen. One cycle cannot exist without the other.

The down cycle is absolutely essential for spiritual realization. You must have failed deeply on some level or experienced some deep loss or pain to be drawn to the spiritual dimension. Or perhaps your very success became empty and meaningless and so turned out to be failure.

Failure lies concealed in every success, and success in every failure. In this world, which is to say on the level of form, everybody "fails" sooner or later, of course, and every achievement eventually comes to naught. All forms are impermanent.

You can still be active and enjoy manifesting and creating new forms and circumstances, but you won't be identified with them. You do not need them to give you a sense of self. They are not your life — only your life situation.

A cycle can last for anything from a few hours to a few years. There are large cycles and small cycles within these large ones. Many illnesses are created through fighting against the cycles of low energy, which are vital for regeneration. The compulsion to do, and the tendency to derive your sense of self-worth and identity from external factors such as achievement, is an inevitable illusion as long as you are identified with the mind.

This makes it hard or impossible for you to accept the low cycles and allow them to be. Thus, the intelligence of the organism may take over as a self-protective measure and create an illness in order to force you to stop, so that the necessary regeneration can take place.

As long as a condition is judged as "good" by your

mind, whether it be a relationship, a possession, a social role, a place, or your physical body, the mind attaches itself to it and identifies with it. It makes you happy, makes you feel good about yourself, and it may become part of who you are or think you are.

But nothing lasts in this dimension where moth and rust consume. Either it ends or it changes, or it may undergo a polarity shift: The same condition that was good yesterday or last year has suddenly or gradually turned into bad. The same condition that made you happy then makes you unhappy. The prosperity of today becomes the empty consumerism of tomorrow. The happy wedding and honeymoon become the unhappy divorce or the unhappy coexistence.

Or a condition disappears, so its absence makes you unhappy. When a condition or situation that the mind has attached itself to and identified with changes or disappears, the mind cannot accept it. It will cling to the disappearing condition and resist the change. It is almost as if a limb were being torn off your body.

This means that your happiness and unhappiness are in fact one. Only the illusion of time separates them.

TO OFFER NO RESISTANCE TO LIFE is to be in a state of grace, ease, and lightness. This state is then no longer dependent upon things being in a certain way, good or bad.

It seems almost paradoxical, yet when your inner dependency on form is gone, the general conditions of your life, the outer forms, tend to improve greatly. Things, people, or conditions that you thought you needed for your happiness now come to you with no struggle or effort on your part, and you are free to enjoy and appreciate them — while they last.

All those things, of course, will still pass away, cycles will come and go, but with dependency gone there is no fear of loss anymore. Life flows with ease.

The happiness that is derived from some secondary source is never very deep. It is only a pale reflection of the joy of Being, the vibrant peace that you find within as you enter the state of nonresistance. Being takes you beyond the polar opposites of the mind and frees you from dependency on form. Even if everything were to collapse and crumble all around you, you would still feel a deep inner core of peace. You may not be happy, but you will be at peace.

∼

USING AND RELINQUISHING NEGATIVITY

All inner resistance is experienced as negativity in one form or another. All negativity is resistance. In this context, the two words are almost synonymous.

Negativity ranges from irritation or impatience to

fierce anger, from a depressed mood or sullen resentment to suicidal despair. Sometimes the resistance triggers the emotional pain-body, in which case even a minor situation may produce intense negativity, such as anger, depression, or deep grief.

The ego believes that through negativity it can manipulate reality and get what it wants. It believes that through it, it can attract a desirable condition or dissolve an undesirable one.

If "you" — the mind — did not believe that unhappiness works, why would you create it? The fact is, of course, that negativity does not work. Instead of attracting a desirable condition, it stops it from arising. Instead of dissolving an undesirable one, it keeps it in place. Its only "useful" function is that it strengthens the ego, and that is why the ego loves it.

Once you have identified with some form of negativity, you do not want to let go, and on a deeply unconscious level, you do not want positive change. It would threaten your identity as a depressed, angry, or hard-done-by person. You will then ignore, deny, or sabotage the positive in your life. This is a common phenomenon. It is also insane.

WATCH ANY PLANT OR ANIMAL AND LET IT TEACH YOU acceptance of what is, surrender to the Now.

Let it teach you Being.

Let it teach you integrity — which means to be one, to be yourself, to be real.

Let it teach you how to live and how to die, and how not to make living and dying into a problem.

Recurring negative emotions do sometimes contain a message, as do illnesses. But any changes that you make, whether they have to do with your work, your relationships, or your surroundings, are ultimately only cosmetic unless they arise out of a change in your level of consciousness. And as far as that is concerned, it can only mean one thing: becoming more present. When you have reached a certain degree of presence, you don't need negativity anymore to tell you what is needed in your life situation.

But as long as negativity is there, use it. Use it as a kind of signal that reminds you to be more present.

WHENEVER YOU FEEL NEGATIVITY ARISING WITHIN YOU, whether caused by an external factor, a thought, or even nothing in particular that you are aware of, look on it as a voice saying, "Attention. Here and Now. Wake up. Get out of your mind. Be present."

Even the slightest irritation is significant and needs to be acknowledged and looked at;

otherwise, there will be a cumulative buildup of unobserved reactions.

You may be able to just drop it once you realize that you don't want to have this energy field inside you and that it serves no purpose. But then make sure that you drop it completely. If you cannot drop it, just accept that it is there and take your attention into the feeling.

AS AN ALTERNATIVE TO DROPPING A NEGATIVE REACTION, you can make it disappear by imagining yourself becoming transparent to the external cause of the reaction.

I recommend that you practice this with little, even trivial, things first. Let's say that you are sitting quietly at home. Suddenly, there is the penetrating sound of a car alarm from across the street. Irritation arises. What is the purpose of the irritation? None whatsoever. Why did you create it? You didn't. The mind did. It was totally automatic, totally unconscious.

Why did the mind create it? Because it holds the unconscious belief that its resistance, which you experience as negativity or unhappiness in some form, will somehow dissolve the undesirable condition. This, of course, is a delusion. The resistance that it creates, the irritation or anger in this case, is far more disturbing than the original cause that it is attempting to dissolve.

All this can be transformed into spiritual practice.

FEEL YOURSELF BECOMING TRANSPARENT, as it
were, without the solidity of a material body.
Now allow the noise, or whatever causes a negative reaction, to pass right through you. It is
no longer hitting a solid "wall" inside you.

As I said, practice with little things first. The car
alarm, the dog barking, the children screaming, the
traffic jam. Instead of having a wall of resistance inside
you that gets constantly and painfully hit by things
that "should not be happening," let everything pass
through you.

Somebody says something to you that is rude or
designed to hurt. Instead of going into unconscious
reaction and negativity, such as attack, defense, or
withdrawal, you let it pass right through you. Offer no
resistance. It is as if there is nobody there to get hurt
anymore. That is forgiveness. In this way, you become
invulnerable.

You can still tell that person that his or her behavior is unacceptable, if that is what you choose to do.
But that person no longer has the power to control
your inner state. You are then in your power — not in
someone else's; nor are you run by your mind. Whether

it is a car alarm, a rude person, a flood, an earthquake, or the loss of all your possessions, the resistance mechanism is the same.

You are still seeking outside, and you cannot get out of the seeking mode. Maybe the next workshop will have the answer, maybe that new technique. To you I would say:

DON'T LOOK FOR PEACE. Don't look for any other state than the one you are in now; otherwise, you will set up inner conflict and unconscious resistance.

Forgive yourself for not being at peace. The moment you completely accept your non-peace, your non-peace becomes transmuted into peace. Anything you accept fully will get you there, will take you into peace. This is the miracle of surrender.

When you accept what is, every moment is the best moment. That is enlightenment.

~

THE NATURE OF COMPASSION

HAVING GONE BEYOND THE MIND-MADE OPPO-SITES, you become like a deep lake. The outer situation of your life, whatever happens there, is the surface of the lake. Sometimes calm, sometimes windy and rough, according to the cycles and seasons. Deep down, however, the lake is always undisturbed. You are the whole lake, not just the surface, and you are in touch with your own depth, which remains absolutely still.

You don't resist change by mentally clinging to any situation. Your inner peace does not depend on it. You abide in Being — unchanging, timeless, deathless — and you are no longer dependent for fulfillment or happiness on the outer world of constantly fluctuating forms. You can enjoy them, play with them, create new forms, appreciate the beauty of it all. But there will be no need to attach yourself to any of it.

As long as you are unaware of Being, the reality of other humans will elude you, because you have not found your own. Your mind will like or dislike their form, which is not just their body but includes their mind as well. True relationship becomes possible only when there is an awareness of Being.

Coming from Being, you will perceive another person's body and mind as just a screen, as it were, behind which you can feel their true reality, as you feel yours. So, when confronted with someone else's suffering or unconscious behavior, you stay present and in touch with Being and are thus able to look beyond the form and feel the other person's radiant and pure Being through your own.

At the level of Being, all suffering is recognized as an illusion. Suffering is due to identification with form. Miracles of healing sometimes occur through this realization, by awakening Being-consciousness in others — if they are ready.

Compassion is the awareness of a deep bond between yourself and all creatures. Next time you say, "I have nothing in common with this person," remember that you have a great deal in common: A few years from now — two years or seventy years, it doesn't make much difference — both of you will have become rotting corpses, then piles of dust, then nothing at all. This is a sobering and humbling realization that leaves little room for pride.

Is this a negative thought? No, it is a fact. Why close your eyes to it? In that sense, there is total equality between you and every other creature.

ONE OF THE MOST POWERFUL SPIRITUAL PRACTICES is to meditate deeply on the mortality of physical forms, including your own. This is called: Die before you die.

Go into it deeply. Your physical form is dissolving, is no more. Then a moment comes when all mind-forms or thoughts also die. Yet you are still there — the divine presence that you are. Radiant, fully awake.

Nothing that was real ever died, only names, forms, and illusions.

At this deep level, compassion becomes healing in the widest sense. In that state, your healing influence is primarily based not on doing but on being. Everybody you come in contact with will be touched by your presence and affected by the peace that you emanate, whether they are conscious of it or not.

When you are fully present and people around you manifest unconscious behavior, you won't feel the need to react to it, so you don't give it any reality. Your peace is so vast and deep that anything that is not peace disappears into it as if it had never existed. This breaks the karmic cycle of action and reaction.

Animals, trees, flowers will feel your peace and respond to it. You teach through being, through demonstrating the peace of God.

You become the "light of the world," an emanation of pure consciousness, and so you eliminate suffering on the level of cause. You eliminate unconsciousness from the world.

~

THE WISDOM OF SURRENDER

It is the quality of your consciousness at this moment that is the main determinant of what kind of future you will experience, so to surrender is the most important thing you can do to bring about positive change. Any action you take is secondary. No truly positive action can arise out of an unsurrendered state of consciousness.

To some people, surrender may have negative connotations, implying defeat, giving up, failing to rise to the challenges of life, becoming lethargic, and so on. True surrender, however, is something entirely different. It does not mean to passively put up with whatever situation you find yourself in and to do nothing about it. Nor does it mean to cease making plans or initiating positive action.

> **SURRENDER IS THE SIMPLE** but profound wisdom of yielding to rather than opposing the flow of life. The only place where you can experience the flow of life is the Now, so to surrender is to accept the present moment unconditionally and without reservation.
>
> It is to relinquish inner resistance to what is.

Inner resistance is to say "no" to what is, through mental judgment and emotional negativity. It becomes particularly pronounced when things "go wrong," which means that there is a gap between the demands or rigid expectations of your mind and what is. That is the pain gap.

If you have lived long enough, you will know that things "go wrong" quite often. It is precisely at those times that surrender needs to be practiced if you want to eliminate pain and sorrow from your life. Acceptance of what is immediately frees you from mind identification and thus reconnects you with Being. Resistance is the mind.

Surrender is a purely inner phenomenon. It does not mean that on the outer level you cannot take action and change the situation.

In fact, it is not the overall situation that you need to accept when you surrender, but just the tiny segment called the Now. For example, if you were stuck in the mud somewhere, you wouldn't say: "Okay, I resign myself to being stuck in the mud." Resignation is not surrender.

YOU DON'T NEED TO ACCEPT AN UNDESIRABLE OR UNPLEASANT LIFE SITUATION. Nor do you need to deceive yourself and say that there is nothing wrong with it. No. You recognize fully that you want to get out of it. You then narrow your attention down to the present moment without mentally labeling it in any way.

This means that there is no judgment of the Now. Therefore, there is no resistance, no emotional negativity. You accept the "isness" of this moment.

Then you take action and do all that you can to get out of the situation.

Such action I call positive action. It is far more effective than negative action, which arises out of anger, despair, or frustration. Until you achieve the desired result, you continue to practice surrender by refraining from labeling the Now.

Let me give you a visual analogy to illustrate the point I am making. You are walking along a path at night, surrounded by a thick fog. But you have a powerful flashlight that cuts through the fog and creates a narrow, clear space in front of you. The fog is your life situation, which includes past and future; the flashlight is your conscious presence; the clear space is the Now.

Non-surrender hardens your psychological form, the shell of the ego, and so creates a strong sense of separateness. The world around you and people in particular come to be perceived as threatening. The unconscious compulsion to destroy others through judgment arises, as does the need to compete and dominate. Even nature becomes your enemy and your perceptions and interpretations are governed by fear. The mental disease that we call paranoia is only a slightly more acute form of this normal but dysfunctional state of consciousness.

Not only your psychological form but also your physical form — your body — becomes hard and rigid through resistance. Tension arises in different parts of the body, and the body as a whole contracts. The free flow of life energy through the body, which is essential for its healthy functioning, is greatly restricted.

Bodywork and certain forms of physical therapy can be helpful in restoring this flow, but unless you practice surrender in your everyday life, those things can only give temporary symptom relief since the cause — the resistance pattern — has not been dissolved.

There is something within you that remains unaffected by the transient circumstances that make up your life situation, and only through surrender do you have access to it. It is your life, your very Being — which exists eternally in the timeless realm of the present.

IF YOU FIND YOUR LIFE SITUATION UNSATISFACTORY or even intolerable, it is only by surrendering first that you can break the unconscious resistance pattern that perpetuates that situation.

Surrender is perfectly compatible with taking action, initiating change, or achieving goals. But in the surrendered state a totally different energy, a different quality, flows into your doing. Surrender reconnects you with the source-energy of Being, and if your doing is infused with Being, it becomes a joyful celebration of life energy that takes you more deeply into the Now.

Through nonresistance, the quality of your consciousness and, therefore, the quality of whatever you are doing or creating is enhanced immeasurably. The results will then look after themselves and reflect that quality. We could call this "surrendered action."

IN THE STATE OF SURRENDER, you see very clearly what needs to be done, and you take action, doing one thing at a time and focusing on one thing at a time.

Learn from nature: See how everything gets accomplished and how the miracle of life unfolds without dissatisfaction or unhappiness.

That's why Jesus said: "Look at the lilies, how they grow; they neither toil nor spin."

IF YOUR OVERALL SITUATION IS UNSATISFACTORY or unpleasant, separate out this instant and surrender to what is. That's the flashlight cutting through the fog. Your state of consciousness then ceases to be controlled by external conditions. You are no longer coming from reaction and resistance.

Then look at the specifics of the situation. Ask yourself, "Is there anything I can do to change the situation, improve it, or remove myself from it?" If so, take appropriate action.

Focus not on the hundred things that you will or may have to do at some future time but on the one thing that you can do now. This doesn't mean you should not do any planning. It may well be that planning is the one thing you can do now. But make sure you don't keep running "mental movies" that continually project yourself into the future, and so lose the Now. Any action you take may not bear fruit immediately. Until it does — do not resist what is.

IF THERE IS NO ACTION YOU CAN TAKE, and you cannot remove yourself from the situation either, then use the situation to make you go more deeply into surrender, more deeply into the Now, more deeply into Being.

When you enter this timeless dimension of the present, change often comes about in strange ways without the need for a great deal of doing on your part. Life becomes helpful and cooperative. If inner factors such as fear, guilt, or inertia prevented you from taking action, they will dissolve in the light of your conscious presence.

Do not confuse surrender with an attitude of "I can't be bothered anymore" or "I just don't care anymore." If you look at it closely, you will find that such an attitude is tainted with negativity in the form of hidden resentment and so is not surrender at all but masked resistance.

As you surrender, direct your attention inward to check if there is any trace of resistance left inside you. Be very alert when you do so; otherwise, a pocket of resistance may continue to hide in some dark corner in the form of a thought or an unacknowledged emotion.

❧

FROM MIND ENERGY TO SPIRITUAL ENERGY

START BY ACKNOWLEDGING THAT THERE IS RESISTANCE. Be there when it happens, when the resistance arises. Observe how your mind creates it, how it labels the situation, yourself, or others. Look at the thought process involved. Feel the energy of the emotion.

By witnessing the resistance, you will see

that it serves no purpose. By focusing all your attention on the Now, the unconscious resistance is made conscious, and that is the end of it.

You cannot be conscious and unhappy, conscious and in negativity. Negativity, unhappiness, or suffering in whatever form means that there is resistance, and resistance is always unconscious,

Would you choose unhappiness? If you did not choose it, how did it arise? What is its purpose? Who is keeping it alive?

Even if you are conscious of your unhappy feelings, the truth is that you are identified with them and keep the process alive through compulsive thinking. All that is unconscious. If you were conscious, that is to say totally present in the Now, all negativity would dissolve almost instantly. It could not survive in your presence. It can only survive in your absence.

Even the pain-body cannot survive for long in your presence. You keep your unhappiness alive by giving it time. That is its lifeblood. Remove time through intense present-moment awareness and it dies. But do you want it to die? Have you truly had enough? Who would you be without it?

Until you practice surrender, the spiritual dimension is something you read about, talk about, get excited about, write books about, think about, believe in — or don't, as the case may be. It makes no difference.

NOT UNTIL YOU SURRENDER does the spiritual dimension become a living reality in your life.

When you do, the energy that you emanate and that then runs your life is of a much higher vibrational frequency than the mind energy that still runs our world.

Through surrender, spiritual energy comes into this world. It creates no suffering for yourself, for other humans, or any other life form on the planet.

∽

SURRENDER IN PERSONAL RELATIONSHIPS

It is true that only an unconscious person will try to use or manipulate others, but it is equally true that only an unconscious person can be used and manipulated. If you resist or fight unconscious behavior in others, you become unconscious yourself.

But surrender doesn't mean that you allow yourself to be used by unconscious people. Not at all. It is perfectly possible to say "no" firmly and clearly to a person or to walk away from a situation and be in a state of complete inner nonresistance at the same time.

WHEN YOU SAY "NO" to a person or a situation, let it come not from reaction but from insight, from a clear realization of what is right or not right for you at that moment.

Let it be a nonreactive "no," a high-quality "no," a "no" that is free of all negativity and so creates no further suffering.

If you cannot surrender, take action immediately: Speak up or do something to bring about a change in the situation — or remove yourself from it. Take responsibility for your life.

Do not pollute your beautiful, radiant inner Being nor the Earth with negativity. Do not give unhappiness in any form whatsoever a dwelling place inside you.

IF YOU CANNOT TAKE ACTION — if you are in prison, for example — then you have two choices left: resistance or surrender. Bondage or inner freedom from external conditions. Suffering or inner peace.

Your relationships will be changed profoundly by surrender. If you can never accept what is, by implication you will not be able to accept anybody the way they are. You will judge, criticize, label, reject, or attempt to change people.

Furthermore, if you continuously make the Now into a means to an end in the future, you will also make every person you encounter or relate with into a means to an end. The relationship — the human being — is then of secondary importance to you, or of no importance at all. What you can get out of the relationship is primary — be it material gain, a sense of power, physical pleasure, or some form of ego gratification.

Let me illustrate how surrender can work in relationships.

WHEN YOU BECOME INVOLVED IN AN ARGUMENT or some conflict situation, perhaps with a partner or someone close to you, start by observing how defensive you become as your own position is attacked, or feel the force of your own aggression as you attack the other person's position.

Observe the attachment to your views and opinions. Feel the mental-emotional energy behind your need to be right and make the other person wrong. That's the energy of the egoic mind. You make it conscious by acknowledging it, by feeling it as fully as possible.

Then one day, in the middle of an argument, you will suddenly realize that you have a choice, and you may decide to drop your own reaction — just to see what happens. You surrender.

I don't mean dropping the reaction just verbally by saying, "Okay, you are right," with a look on your face that says, "I am above all this childish unconsciousness." That's just displacing the resistance to another level, with the egoic mind still in charge, claiming superiority. I am speaking of letting go of the entire mental-emotional energy field inside you that was fighting for power.

The ego is cunning, so you have to be very alert, very present, and totally honest with yourself to see whether you have truly relinquished your identification with a mental position and so freed yourself from your mind.

IF YOU SUDDENLY FEEL VERY LIGHT, CLEAR, AND DEEPLY AT PEACE, that is an unmistakable sign that you have truly surrendered. Then observe what happens to the other person's mental position as you no longer energize it through resistance. When identification with mental positions is out of the way, true communication begins.

Nonresistance doesn't necessarily mean doing nothing. All it means is that any "doing" becomes nonreactive. Remember the deep wisdom underlying the practice of Eastern martial arts: Don't resist the opponent's force. Yield to overcome.

Having said that, "doing nothing" when you are in a state of intense presence is a very powerful transformer and healer of situations and people.

It is radically different from inactivity in the ordinary state of consciousness, or rather unconsciousness, which stems from fear, inertia, or indecision. The real "doing nothing" implies inner nonresistance and intense alertness.

On the other hand, if action is required, you will no longer react from your conditioned mind, but you will respond to the situation out of your conscious presence. In that state, your mind is free of concepts, including the concept of nonviolence. So who can predict what you will do?

The ego believes that in your resistance lies your strength, whereas in truth resistance cuts you off from Being, the only place of true power. Resistance is weakness and fear masquerading as strength. What the ego sees as weakness is your Being in its purity, innocence, and power. What it sees as strength is weakness. So the ego exists in a continuous resistance mode and plays counterfeit roles to cover up your "weakness," which in truth is your power.

Until there is surrender, unconscious role-playing constitutes a large part of human interaction. In surrender, you no longer need ego defenses and false masks. You become very simple, very real. "That's dangerous," says the ego. "You'll get hurt. You'll become vulnerable."

What the ego doesn't know, of course, is that only through the letting go of resistance, through becoming "vulnerable," can you discover your true and essential invulnerability.

NINE

~

Transforming Illness and Suffering

TRANSFORMING ILLNESS INTO ENLIGHTENMENT

Surrender is inner acceptance of what is without any reservations. We are talking about your life — this instant — not the conditions or circumstances of your life, not what I call your life situation.

Illness is part of your life situation. As such, it has a past and a future. Past and future form an uninterrupted continuum, unless the redeeming power of the Now is activated through your conscious presence. As you know, underneath the various conditions that make up your life situation, which exists in time, there is something deeper, more essential: your Life, your very Being in the timeless Now.

As there are no problems in the Now, there is no illness either. The belief in a label that someone attaches to your condition keeps the condition in place, empowers it, and makes a seemingly solid reality out of a temporary imbalance. It gives it not only reality and solidity but also continuity in time that it did not have before.

BY FOCUSING ON THIS INSTANT and refraining from labeling it mentally, illness is reduced to one or several of these factors: physical pain, weakness, discomfort, or disability. That is what you surrender to — now. You do not surrender to the idea of "illness."

Allow the suffering to force you into the present moment, into a state of intense conscious presence. Use it for enlightenment.

Surrender does not transform what is, at least not directly. Surrender transforms you. When you are transformed, your whole world is transformed, because the world is only a reflection.

Illness is not the problem. You are the problem — as long as the egoic mind is in control.

WHEN YOU ARE ILL OR DISABLED, do not feel that you have failed in some way, do not feel guilty. Do not blame life for treating you unfairly, but do not blame yourself either. All that is resistance.

If you have a major illness, use it for enlightenment. Anything "bad" that happens in your life — use it for enlightenment.

Withdraw time from the illness. Do not give it any past or future. Let it force you into intense present-moment awareness — and see what happens.

Become an alchemist. Transmute base metal into gold, suffering into consciousness, disaster into enlightenment.

Are you seriously ill and feeling angry now about what I have just said? Then that is a clear sign that the illness has become part of your sense of self and that you are now protecting your identity — as well as protecting the illness.

The condition that is labeled "illness" has nothing to do with who you truly are.

Whenever any kind of disaster strikes, or something goes seriously "wrong" — illness, disability, loss of home or fortune or of a socially defined identity, breakup of a close relationship, death or suffering of a loved one, or your own impending death — know that there is another side to it, that you are just one step away from something incredible: a complete alchemical transmutation of the base metal of pain and suffering into gold. That one step is called surrender.

I do not mean to say that you will become happy in such a situation. You will not. But fear and pain will become transmuted into an inner peace and serenity that come from a very deep place — from the Unmanifested itself. It is "the peace of God, which passes all understanding." Compared to that, happiness is quite a shallow thing.

With this radiant peace comes the realization — not on the level of mind but within the depth of your Being — that you are indestructible, immortal. This is not a belief. It is absolute certainty that needs no external evidence or proof from some secondary source.

∾

TRANSFORMING SUFFERING INTO PEACE

In certain extreme situations, it may still be impossible for you to accept the Now. But you always get a second chance at surrender.

YOUR FIRST CHANCE IS TO SURRENDER each moment to the reality of that moment. Knowing that what is cannot be undone — because it already is — you say yes to what is or accept what isn't.

Then you do what you have to do, whatever the situation requires.

If you abide in this state of acceptance, you create no more negativity, no more suffering, no more unhappiness. You then live in a state of nonresistance, a state of grace and lightness, free of struggle.

Whenever you are unable to do that, whenever you miss that chance — either because you are not generating enough conscious presence to prevent some habitual and unconscious resistance pattern from arising, or because the condition is so extreme as to be absolutely unacceptable to you — then you are creating some form of pain, some form of suffering.

It may look as if the situation is creating the suffering, but ultimately this is not so — your resistance is.

NOW HERE IS YOUR SECOND CHANCE AT SURRENDER: If you cannot accept what is outside, then accept what is inside. If you cannot accept the external condition, accept the internal condition.

This means: Do not resist the pain. Allow

it to be there. Surrender to the grief, despair, fear, loneliness, or whatever form the suffering takes. Witness it without labeling it mentally. Embrace it.

Then see how the miracle of surrender transmutes deep suffering into deep peace. This is your crucifixion. Let it become your resurrection and ascension.

When your pain is deep, all talk of surrender will probably seem futile and meaningless anyway. When your pain is deep, you will likely have a strong urge to escape from it rather than surrender to it. You don't want to feel what you feel. What could be more normal? But there is no escape, no way out.

There are many pseudo escapes — work, drink, drugs, anger, projection, suppression, and so on — but they don't free you from the pain. Suffering does not diminish in intensity when you make it unconscious. When you deny emotional pain, everything you do or think as well as your relationships become contaminated with it. You broadcast it, so to speak, as the energy you emanate, and others will pick it up subliminally.

If they are unconscious, they may even feel compelled to attack or hurt you in some way, or you may hurt them in an unconscious projection of your pain.

You attract and manifest whatever corresponds to your inner state.

WHEN THERE IS NO WAY OUT, THERE IS STILL ALWAYS A WAY THROUGH. So don't turn away from the pain. Face it. Feel it fully. Feel it — don't think about it! Express it if necessary, but don't create a script in your mind around it. Give all your attention to the feeling, not to the person, event, or situation that seems to have caused it.

Don't let the mind use the pain to create a victim identity for yourself out of it. Feeling sorry for yourself and telling others your story will keep you stuck in suffering.

Since it is impossible to get away from the feeling, the only possibility of change is to move into it; otherwise, nothing will shift.

So give your complete attention to what you feel, and refrain from mentally labeling it. As you go into the feeling, be intensely alert.

At first, it may seem like a dark and terrifying place, and when the urge to turn away from it comes, observe it but don't act on it. Keep putting your attention on the pain, keep feeling the grief, the fear, the dread, the loneliness, whatever it is.

Stay alert, stay present — present with your whole Being, with every cell of your body. As you do so, you are bringing a light into this darkness. This is the flame of your consciousness.

At this stage, you don't need to be concerned with surrender anymore. It has happened already. How? Full attention is full acceptance, is surrender. By giving full attention, you use the power of the Now, which is the power of your presence.

No hidden pocket of resistance can survive in it. Presence removes time. Without time, no suffering, no negativity, can survive.

THE ACCEPTANCE OF SUFFERING is a journey into death. Facing deep pain, allowing it to be, taking your attention into it, is to enter death consciously. When you have died this death, you realize that there is no death — and there is nothing to fear. Only the ego dies.

Imagine a ray of sunlight that has forgotten it is an inseparable part of the sun and deludes itself into believing it has to fight for survival and create and cling to an identity other than the sun. Would the death of this delusion not be incredibly liberating?

DO YOU WANT AN EASY DEATH? Would you rather die without pain, without agony? Then die to the past every moment, and let the light of your presence shine away the heavy, time-bound self you thought of as "you."

~

THE WAY OF THE CROSS —
ENLIGHTENMENT THROUGH SUFFERING

The way of the cross is the old way to enlightenment, and until recently it was the only way. But don't dismiss it or underestimate its efficacy. It still works.

The way of the cross is a complete reversal. It means that the worst thing in your life, your cross, turns into the best thing that ever happened to you, by forcing you into surrender, into "death," forcing you to become as nothing, to become as God — because God, too, is no-thing.

Enlightenment through suffering — the way of the cross — means to be forced into the kingdom of heaven kicking and screaming. You finally surrender because you can't stand the pain anymore, but the pain could go on for a long time until this happens.

ENLIGHTENMENT CONSCIOUSLY CHOSEN means to relinquish your attachment to past and future and to make the Now the main focus of your life.

It means choosing to dwell in the state of presence rather than in time.

It means saying yes to what is.

You then don't need pain anymore.

How much more time do you think you will need before you are able to say, "I will create no more pain, no more suffering?" How much more pain do you need before you can make that choice?

If you think that you need more time, you will get more time — and more pain. Time and pain are inseparable.

∼

THE POWER TO CHOOSE

Choice implies consciousness — a high degree of consciousness. Without it, you have no choice. Choice begins the moment you disidentify from the mind and its conditioned patterns, the moment you become present.

Until you reach that point, you are unconscious, spiritually speaking. This means that you are compelled to think, feel, and act in certain ways according to the conditioning of your mind.

Nobody chooses dysfunction, conflict, pain. Nobody chooses insanity. They happen because there is not enough presence in you to dissolve the past, not enough light to dispel the darkness. You are not fully here. You have not quite woken up yet. In the meantime, the conditioned mind is running your life.

Similarly, if you are one of the many people who have an issue with their parents, if you still harbor resentment about something they did or did not do, then you still believe that they had a choice — that they could have acted differently. It always looks as if people had a choice, but that is an illusion. As long as your mind with its conditioned patterns runs your life, as long as you are your mind, what choice do you have? None. You are not even there. The mind-identified state is severely dysfunctional. It is a form of insanity.

Almost everyone is suffering from this illness in varying degrees. The moment you realize this, there can be no more resentment. How can you resent someone's illness? The only appropriate response is compassion.

If you are run by your mind, although you have no choice you will still suffer the consequences of your unconsciousness, and you will create further suffering. You will bear the burden of fear, conflict, problems, and pain. The suffering thus created will eventually force you out of your unconscious state.

YOU CANNOT TRULY FORGIVE YOURSELF or others as long as you derive your sense of self from the past. Only through accessing the power of the Now, which is your own power, can there be true forgiveness. This renders the past powerless, and you realize deeply that nothing you ever did or that was ever done to you could touch even in the slightest the radiant essence of who you are.

When you surrender to what is and so become fully present, the past ceases to have any power. You do not need it anymore. Presence is the key. The Now is the key.

Since resistance is inseparable from the mind, relinquishment of resistance — surrender — is the end of the mind as your master, the impostor pretending to be "you," the false god. All judgment and all negativity dissolve.

The realm of Being, which had been obscured by the mind, then opens up.

Suddenly, a great stillness arises within you, an unfathomable sense of peace.

And within that peace, there is great joy.

And within that joy, there is love.

And at the innermost core, there is the sacred, the immeasurable, That which cannot be named.

ACKNOWLEDGMENTS

I am grateful to Victoria Ritchie, Connie Kellough, Marc Allen and the staff at New World Library for their support and superb editing of this book.

My special thanks to all those individuals who helped promote and support *The Power of Now* in its early stages. Only some them are mentioned here. Cathy Bordi, Marina Borusso, Randall Bradley, Ginna Bell-Bragg, Tommy Chan, Greg Clifford, Steve Coe, Barbara Dempsey, Kim Eng, Doug France, Joyce Franzee, Remi Frumkin, Wilma Fuchs, Stephen Gawtry, Pat Gordon, Matthew and Joan Greenblatt, Jane Griffith, Surati Haarbrucker, Marilyn Knipp, Nora Morin, Karen McPhee, Sandy Neufeld, Jim Nowak, Carey Parder,

Carmen Priolo, Usha Raetze, Joseph Roberts, Steve Ross, Sarah Runyen, Nikki Sachdeva, Spar Street, Marshall and Barbara Thurber, Brock Tully.

I would like to express my love and gratitude to the owners and staff of the many privately owned bookstores that have been instrumental in getting *The Power of Now* out into the world. You are doing wonderful work! My special thanks go to:

Banyen Books, Vancouver, BC
East-West Bookshop, Seattle, WA
East-West Bookshop, Mountain View, CA
Greenhouse Books, Vancouver, BC
Heaven on Earth Book Store, Encinitas, CA
New Age Books & Crystals, Calgary, AB
Open Secret Book Store, San Rafael, CA
Thunderbird Book Store, Carmel, CA
Transitions Bookplace, Chicago, IL
Watkins Bookshop, London, UK

RECOMMENDED RESOURCES

The Power of Now by Eckhart Tolle (Hodder & Stoughton, 2001). Already on its way to becoming classic. The complete book is also on audio.

The Power of Now Companion Audio by Eckhart Tolle (Hodder & Stoughton, 2002).

An Open Heart by the Dalai Lama, edited by Nicholas Vreeland (Hodder & Stoughton, 2001).

The Last Hours of Ancient Sunlight by Thom Hartmann (Hodder & Stoughton, 2001).

The Prophet's Way by Thom Hartmann (Hodder Mobius, 2002).

The Spiritual Teachings of Marcus Aurelius by Mark Forstater (Hodder & Stoughton, 2000).

The Spiritual Teachings of the Tao by Mark Forstater (Hodder & Stoughton, 2001).

The Spiritual Teachings of Seneca by Mark Forstater and Victoria Radin (Hodder & Stoughton, 2001).

ECKHART TOLLE TV

At this time of accelerating transformation, in response to what he calls "the evolutionary impulse," Eckhart Tolle will be teaching in a pioneering new format: monthly webcasts designed to catalyze spiritual awakening, foster community, and provide clarity, guidance, and support. Now you have the opportunity to join people across the globe to experience Eckhart's life-changing teachings. As a member of Eckhart Tolle TV, you'll have the opportunity to submit questions to Eckhart, participate in live recordings, view monthly talks by Eckhart, receive weekly Present Moment Reminders, join online group meditations, and more. To start watching or to learn more, please visit

www.EckhartTolleTV.com